UP THE
KOYUKUK

Volume 10, Number 4, 1983
ALASKA GEOGRAPHIC®

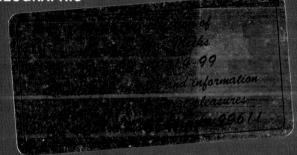

The Alaska Geographic Society

To teach many more to better know and use our natural resources

---

Chief Editor: Robert A. Henning
Assistant Chief Editor: Barbara Olds
Editor: Penny Rennick
Editorial Assistant: Kathy Doogan
Designer: Sandra Harner
Maps: Jon.Hersh

About This Issue:

Alaska's remote Koyukuk River drainage, while perhaps not as well known as other parts of the state, still reflects most of the ingredients of the Alaska way of life: fishing, trapping, hunting, mining, outdoor recreation, and the beginnings of contemporary commerce and development. For an overview of this microcosm, we called upon Bill Sherwonit, a geologist with many seasons' experience in the Koyukuk. Terrence Cole of The *ALASKA JOURNAL®* staff provides a review of the region's early mining history; and Tishu Ulen, born and raised in Koyukuk country, describes the ways of her people, the Kobuk Eskimos of the upper Koyukuk. Shirley English and Walter Johnson, whose experience with the Koyukuk goes back many years, contribute insights into some of the people and events that made history in the region, and Joseph Agnese gives us a glimpse into the activities of a fish camp along the Koyukuk River.

We thank the many photographers whose fine photos help capture the special feeling of Koyukuk country; and we are grateful to reviewers, especially Gil Mull and Tom Bundtzen, for their comments.

Editor's note: Population figures are from the Alaska Department of Community and Regional Affairs' state revenue sharing statistics except for the population figure for Bettles, which is from the 1980 census.

ALASKA GEOGRAPHIC®, ISSN 0361-1353, is published quarterly by The Alaska Geographic Society, Anchorage, Alaska 99509-6057. Second-class postage paid in Edmonds, Washington 98020-3588. Printed in U.S.A.

THE ALASKA GEOGRAPHIC SOCIETY is a nonprofit organization exploring new frontiers of knowledge across the lands of the polar rim, learning how other men and other countries live in their Norths, putting the geography book back in the classroom, exploring new methods of teaching and learning — sharing in the excitement of discovery in man's wonderful new world north of 51°16'.

MEMBERS OF THE SOCIETY RECEIVE *Alaska Geographic®*, a quality magazine which devotes each quarterly issue to monographic in-depth coverage of a northern geographic region or resource-oriented subject.

MEMBERSHIP DUES in The Alaska Geographic Society are $30 per year; $34 to non-U.S. addresses. (Eighty percent of each year's dues is for a one-year subscription to *Alaska Geographic®*.) Order from The Alaska Geographic Society, Box 4-EEE, Anchorage, Alaska 99509-6057; (907) 274-0521.

MATERIAL SOUGHT: The editors of *Alaska Geographic®* seek a wide variety of informative material on the lands north of 51°16' on geographic subjects — anything to do with resources and their uses (with heavy emphasis on quality color photography) — from Alaska, Northern Canada, Siberia, Japan — all geographic areas that have a relationship to Alaska in a physical or economic sense. We do not want material done in excessive scientific terminology. A query to the editors is suggested. Payments are made for all material upon publication.

CHANGE OF ADDRESS: The post office does not automatically forward *Alaska Geographic®* when you move. To insure continous service, notify us six weeks before moving. Send us your new address and zip code (and moving date), your old address and zip code, and if possible send a mailing label from a copy of *Alaska Geographic®*. Send this information to *Alaska Geographic®* Mailing Offices, 130 Second Avenue South, Edmonds, Washington 98020-3588.

MAILING LISTS: We have begun making our members' names and addresses available to carefully screened publications and companies whose products and activities might be of interest to you. If you would prefer not to receive such mailings, please so advise us, and include your mailing label (or your name and address if label is not available).

Library of Congress cataloging in publication data:
Main entry under title:
Up the Koyukuk.
  (Alaska geographic, ISSN 0361-1353; v. 10, no. 4)
  1. Koyukuk River Valley (Alaska) — Social life and customs — Addresses, essays, lectures. 2. Koyukuk River Valley (Alaska) — Biography — Addresses, essays, lectures. 3. Koyukuk River Valley (Alaska) — Description and travel — Addresses, essays, lectures. I. Alaska Geographic Society. II. Series.
F901.A266   vol. 10, no. 4 [F912.K67]   917.98s   83-15343
ISBN 0-88240-200-5   [917.98'6]

(The cover) *The mining village of Wiseman spreads out along a bend of the Middle Fork of the Koyukuk River. Peaks of the Endicott Mountains of the Brooks Range rise in the distance.* (Steve McCutcheon)

(Previous page) *Yellow leaves of this lone birch stand out in stark contrast to the color of the snow-frosted landscape in the Alatna River Valley on the north side of the Koyukuk.* (Shelley Schneider)

(Opposite →) *Clouds float over the lower Koyukuk River near Niitltoktalogi Mountain (2,050 feet) about 32 miles north northwest of Hughes.* (Jim Yuskavitch)

A canoeist and her dog enjoy the beauty of Iniakuk Lake, 40 miles northwest of Allakaket. The lake drains into the Malamute Fork of the Alatna River, whose waters eventually reach the Koyukuk near Allakaket. (Kit Marrs)

The Koyukuk River Basin

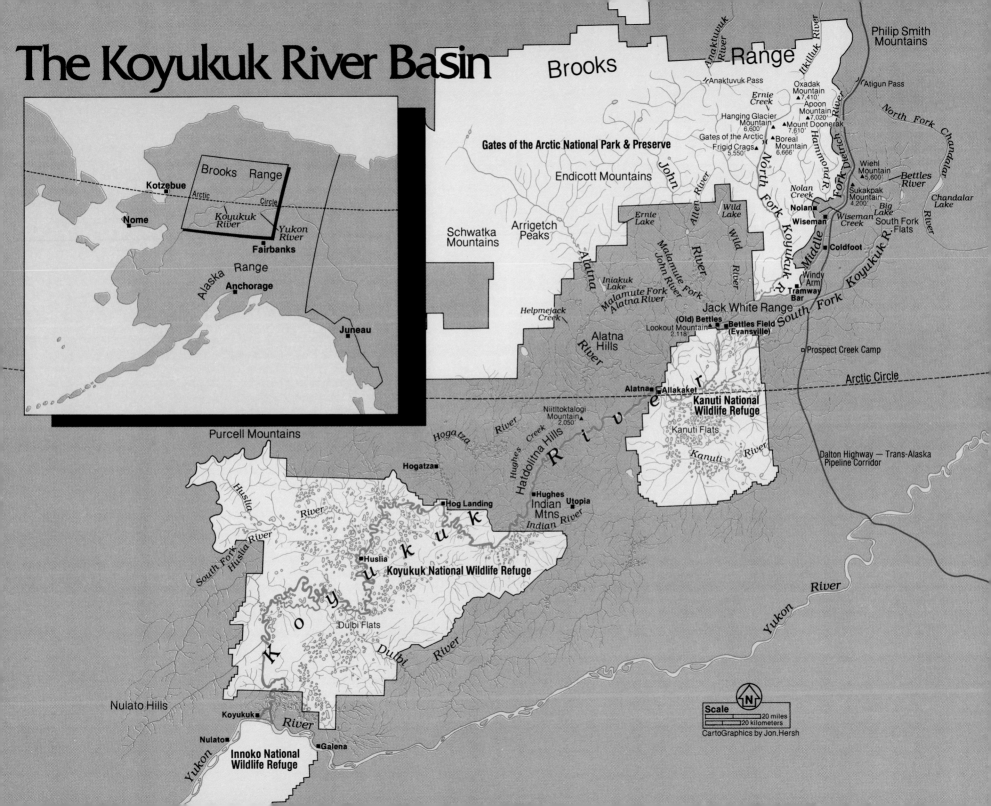

Brooks Range
Philip Smith Mountains

Brooks Range

Kotzebue

Arctic

Circle

Koyukuk River

Yukon River

Nome

Fairbanks

Alaska Range

Anchorage

Juneau

Anaktuvuk River
Itkilluk River

Anaktuvuk Pass

Oxadak Mountain 7,410'
Atigun Pass

Ernie Creek

Apoon Mountain 7,020'

Gates of the Arctic National Park & Preserve

Hanging Glacier Mountain 6,600'
Mount Doonerak 7,610'
North Fork Chandalar

Gates of the Arctic
Boreal Mountain 6,666'

Frigid Crags 5,550'

Endicott Mountains

John River

Wiehl Mountain 5,600'

Bettles River

Nolan Creek

Chandalar Lake

Arrigetch Peaks

Schwatka Mountains

Ernie Lake

Wild Lake

Nolan

Sukakpak Mountain 4,200'

Big Lake

Allen River

Malamute Fork John River

Wiseman

Wiseman Creek

South Fork Flats

Alatna River

Wild River

Middle Fork Koyukuk R.

Coldfoot

Iniakuk Lake

Helpmejack Creek

Malamute Fork Alatna River

Windy Arm

Tramway Bar

Jack White Range

North Fork Koyukuk R.

South Fork Koyukuk R.

Alatna Hills

(Old) Bettles
Lookout Mountain 2,118'
Bettles Field (Evansville)

Prospect Creek Camp

Alatna River

Purcell Mountains

Niitltoktalogi Mountain 2,050'

Alatna

Allakaket

Kanuti National Wildlife Refuge

Arctic Circle

Hogatza River

Hughes Creek

Koyukuk River

Kanuti Flats

Dalton Highway — Trans-Alaska Pipeline Corridor

Hogatza

Hatdolitna Hills

Kanuti River

Huslia River

Hog Landing

Hughes
Indian Mtns
Utopia
Indian River

South Fork Huslia River

Koyukuk

Huslia

Koyukuk National Wildlife Refuge

Yukon River

Dulbi Flats

Nulato Hills

Dulbi River

Koyukuk

Scale
20 miles
20 kilometers

CartoGraphics by Jon.Hersh

Koyukuk

River

Nulato

Galena

Yukon

Innoko National Wildlife Refuge

Koyukuk Country

By Bill Sherwonit

Editor's note: *After having spent several seasons exploring Koyukuk country as a geologist, Bill Sherwonit is now a reporter for* The Anchorage Times.

The Koyukuk River is born among the peaks and valleys of the Brooks Range, Alaska's northernmost chain of mountains. From its birthplace nearly 100 miles north of the Arctic Circle, the Koyukuk flows south and west for 554 miles.

The state's third largest river and eighth largest in discharge finally reaches maturity and old age in the foothills and tundra lowlands of central Alaska, where it meanders toward its meeting with the Yukon River.

But long before joining the Yukon, the Koyukuk spends a wild youth flowing through the Endicott Mountains of the central Brooks Range. This approximately 600-mile chain spans the entire width of arctic Alaska and is divided into several mountain provinces. The Endicott Mountains are bordered on the west and southwest by the Schwatka Mountains and on the northeast by the Philip Smith Mountains.

However, the Koyukuk is not "a" river — at least not until it has left the Endicotts far behind. Within the Brooks Range, the Koyukuk consists of three branches: the North, Middle, and South forks. And each of the branches spends its youth in a vastly different environment.

The North Fork of the Koyukuk originates among precipitous mountains and steep, alpine gorges that form the south side of the continental divide, at an elevation of about 4,000 feet. Surrounding peaks commonly rise to heights of 6,000 feet or more.

On the opposite side of the divide, the Itkillik and Nanuskuk rivers flow northward toward the

Lifeline of Koyukuk country, the mighty Koyukuk River weaves its way for more than 550 miles across northcentral Alaska from its birthplace in the Brooks Range to its mouth at the village of Koyukuk on the Yukon River. (Kit Marrs)

Arctic Ocean; the North Fork, meanwhile, flows south toward the mighty Yukon River which eventually empties into the Bering Sea.

South of its headwaters, the North Fork passes Mount Doonerak (7,610 feet), tallest peak within the Koyukuk drainage. Robert Marshall, U.S. Forest Service official who explored extensively in the central Brooks Range in the early decades of the twentieth century, first called the jagged spire of Doonerak the "Matterhorn of the Koyukuk," and described the peak as a "towering, black unscalable-looking giant."

The North Fork then flows past dozens of peaks and creeks explored and named by Marshall, including 5,550-foot Frigid Crags and 6,666-foot Boreal Mountain, the original "Gates of the Arctic" which Marshall said form "two stupendous walls" on either side of the Koyukuk Valley.

From its source along the arctic divide, the North Fork winds its way more than 120 miles through the Brooks Range before finally joining forces with the Middle Fork in the marshy tundra flats south of the Endicotts.

The Middle Fork begins at the confluence of the Dietrich and Bettles rivers, about 60 miles southeast of the North Fork headwaters and 30 miles south of the divide. Both rivers that join to create the Middle Fork are large, braided streams that flow through wide, flat glacial valleys three or more miles wide. At their junction, Sukakpak (4,200 feet) and Wiehl (5,600 feet) mountains — massive gray limestone peaks with sheer cliffs — rise precipitously above low, rounded hills and plateaulike benches.

From the river's beginning among hills and mountains of limestone and marble, the Middle

One of the highest points in Koyukuk country, Mount Doonerak (7,610 feet) rises north of Wiseman near the headwaters of the North Fork Koyukuk.
(Jon Nickles)

Fork, paralleled by the trans-Alaska pipeline and haul road, soon passes into "gold country."

Mountains of metamorphic schist and phyllite rise as high as 5,900 feet, but most of the somber gray, brown, and black peaks stand no higher than 4,000 feet. Placer gold deposits, derived from quartz veins with the schists, are common along the Middle Fork and its tributaries.

While the North Fork descends more than 3,000 feet during its trip through the Endicotts, from 4,000 feet at its source to less than 1,000 feet at the southern limits of the range, the Middle Fork drops only about 200 feet, from 1,200 to 1,000 feet.

Unlike the North Fork, born among steep, rugged mountains with imposing vertical cliffs and deep gorges, the South Fork has its origins among the subdued foothills of the southeastern Endicott Mountains. This is no roaring mountain stream with rushing rapids and braided channels; this river meanders past rounded hills and mountains, through the South Fork Flats into a tundra lowland of spruce and birch, with hundreds of small lakes and ponds. At its headwaters, the South Fork Valley has an elevation of about 1,800 feet; summits of surrounding peaks rarely reach more than 5,000 feet.

Despite the mountainous terrain, the over-whelming feeling gained from the central Brooks Range is one of wide-open spaces. Contributing to this feeling are the expanses of low rolling hills and flat, plateaulike benches interspersed with the steeper, more rugged peaks. This openness is accentuated by the general absence of forests. Even in the southernmost portions of the range, the tree line stands at 2,000 to 3,000 feet. Hence most of the mountainous terrain is bare rock or is covered by a thin veneer of alpine tundra meadows.

This roost in the Endicott Mountains, northern wall of Koyukuk country, affords hikers a splendid view of the knife-edged Arrigetch Peaks. (Mark McDermott)

To the north, forests of birch and stunted spruce gradually become restricted to valley bottoms. Eventually the trees reach their northern limit and the arctic forests end, leaving only stands of scrub brush and expanses of arctic grass.

For the most part, Pleistocene glaciation, when most of the Brooks Range was covered by a large glacial mass, created this wide-open feeling. Although few glaciers remain in portions of the Endicott Mountains through which the Koyukuk forks flow, large ice masses are present north of the arctic divide as well as in the Schwatka Mountains to the west and the Franklin and Romanzof mountains to the northeast.

Glaciers that once covered the range have left their undeniable imprint on the landscape of the Endicotts. Creeks flow through U-shaped alpine valleys; wide circular basins, known as cirques, surrounded by knife-edged ridges, known as arêtes, have been sculpted into the mountains; deep blue or blue-green lakes sit in upper reaches of many valleys.

The section of the Endicotts through which the Koyukuk flows is underlain by a sequence of Paleozoic (250 to 570 million years old) sedimentary and volcanic rocks which have been metamorphosed and subjected to intense deformation.

The majority of the rocks in the southern Brooks Range developed in the Devonian subdivision of the Paleozoic, 365 to 405 million years ago. At that time, clastic sedimentary rocks, such as sandstones, shales, and graywackes, plus accompanying volcanics were deposited in active basins along the margins of the North American continent. Intermittent emergence and submergence produced a repeated series of rock types. To the north, extensive carbonate sequences of limestone and dolomite were formed on a shallow water platform. The rocks were metamorphosed during a major tectonic event that occurred in late Jurassic or Cretaceous time, 67 to 160 million years ago. At this time the rocks were subjected to large-scale thrust faulting, recumbent folding, and intrusion of large igneous bodies.

Based on mineral assemblages and degree of metamorphism, the Paleozoic rocks within the Endicotts can be divided into two east-west trending belts, one schist and one carbonate, which extend for more than 500 miles along the southern Brooks Range.

The schist belt is most commonly 20 to 40 miles wide although locally it can be considerably wider. Rocks in this belt are typically low-grade in metamorphism but are severely deformed by folding and faulting. The carbonate belt lies to the north. Most prominent unit within the belt is the Skajit Limestone, a light-to-dark-gray, banded-to-massive unit that forms distinctive cliffs. The carbonate sequence includes minor dolomite, schist, and greenstone. A younger series of shales, slates, quartzites, conglomerates, and phyllites overlie the carbonate sequence. The schist and carbonate belts act as hosts for several types of metallic mineral deposits.

Massive sulfide deposits of copper-lead-zinc-silver have been found within the metavolcanic rocks that occur near the top of the schist belt. The richest of these deposits occurs west of the Endicotts in the Ambler mineral district. Deposits with possible economic potential are also associated with metavolcanic rocks to the east in the Chandalar copper belt.

The carbonate belt, particularly the Skajit Limestone and associated dolomite, contains copper deposits and lead-zinc-silver deposits. None of these metallic mineral deposits within the Koyukuk region have thus far been developed commercially. Only gold has been mined extensively.

Soon after the three forks come together in the lowlands south of the Brooks Range, the Koyukuk passes between the Alatna Hills and the Jack White Range. These low, rounded mountains whose elevations rarely exceed 3,000 feet, are underlain

Aufeis, formed partly because of stream constriction by culverts along the Dalton Highway, lines Douglas Creek, a tributary of the South Fork Koyukuk. The trans-Alaska pipeline crosses the South Fork at about milepost 156 on the run from Livengood in Alaska's Interior to Prudhoe Bay on the arctic coast. (Jon Nickles)

Bill (left) and David Trudeau walk down the North Fork Koyukuk with Mount Doonerak (left) and Hanging Glacier Mountain (6,600 feet) behind them. (Jon Nickles)

(Left ←) Blue-green malachite, a copper ore, is visible in these metavolcanic rocks of the Chandalar copper belt to the east of the Middle Fork Koyukuk Valley. (Bill Sherwonit)

(Right →) Composed of marble, these peaks tower above the valley of the Bettles River which, with the Dietrich River, forms the Middle Fork of the Koyukuk. (Bill Sherwonit)

Will Miles (left), Kathryn Dahl, and Bill and David Trudeau hike across the alpine tundra of Ernie Pass, a 3,200-foot breach in the continental divide which separates the north-flowing waters of the Anaktuvuk River from the south-flowing tributaries of the North Fork Koyukuk. (Jon Nickles)

by Jurassic-Cretaceous mafic volcanics and intrusive rocks with associated assemblages of sedimentary graywacke and mudstone.

The Koyukuk then enters Kanuti Flats and follows a convoluted path through the broad tundra lowland with its abundance of marshes and thousands of lakes and ponds.

Once beyond the flats, the river heads west into another region of low, rounded, heavily vegetated hills, passing between the Indian Mountains and the Hatdolitna Hills. These hills, generally below 2,500 feet, are also underlain by Mezozoic (67 to 250 million years old) rocks of graywackes, mudstones, volcanics (andesites and basalts), plus a group of granitic intrusives that include granodiorite and quartz monzonite.

The final leg of the Koyukuk's journey to the Yukon is spent in another lowland basin characterized by extreme flatness, wide expanses of tundra meadows and marshes, and the ubiquitous lakes and ponds. In its lowermost reaches, the Koyukuk is bordered on the west by the Nulato Hills, about 1,000 to 2,000 feet in elevation, which consist of Cretaceous sedimentary rocks such as graywacke, shale, and conglomerate.

Climate

From its headwaters to its meeting with the Yukon, the Koyukuk flows through Alaska's continental climate zone. This zone, which includes most of interior Alaska and extends from the arctic divide on the north to the Alaska Range and Kuskokwim Mountains on the south, is characterized by extremes in temperature — hot summers and very cold winters — plus light precipitation.

Mean annual snowfall throughout most of the Koyukuk drainage averages from 60 to 80 inches. Total annual precipitation, most of which occurs in late summer and early fall as rainstorms, is generally less than 30 inches.

The region experiences more than a 100° F difference in temperatures between summer highs and winter lows. July is the warmest month, January the coldest. Temperatures change very little from the Brooks Range to the Yukon. At Wiseman, in the Brooks Range, average summer temperatures range from 36° to 68°, although readings have soared as high as 90°. Winter temperatures average from minus 20° to plus 18°, but have reached as low as minus 65°. Similarly, Nulato, 300 miles to the southwest on the Yukon near the mouth of the Koyukuk, has summer temperatures which average from 37° to 69°, while winter ranges from minus 16° to plus 20°. The lowest temperature recorded in Alaska was taken

Coldest temperature ever recorded for Alaska, minus 80°, was measured at Prospect Creek Camp, a trans-Alaska pipeline construction camp not far from the South Fork Koyukuk. (Gil Mull)

15

within the Koyukuk drainage when the mercury dropped to minus 80° at Prospect Creek Camp, about 25 miles southeast of Bettles, on January 23, 1971.

Breakup of the Koyukuk, as far south as Hughes, occurs in early May, while freezeup takes place in mid- to late October. The Koyukuk is iced up for more than 200 days of the year.

Flora

The upper Koyukuk drainage marks the northernmost limit of Alaska's forests. Three types of spruce-hardwood forests, bottomland, lowland, and upland, occur within the area. Bottomland forests are characterized by tall stands of white spruce and poplar in river bottoms, and high and low shrubs such as alder, willow, and berry plants.

Lowland forests consist of black spruce or mixtures of black spruce with tamarack, birch, aspen, and poplar scattered throughout the lowlands south of the Brooks Range. Interspersed with the trees are willows, lowbush cranberries, blueberries, mosses, grasses, cotton grass, and ferns.

Upland forests of white and/or black spruce with scattered stands of birch and aspen cover the mountains and foothills of the Brooks Range from 2,000 to 3,000 feet. Black spruce is most common on north-facing slopes and poorly drained flat areas. Mosses, berry plants, willows, alders, and dwarf birch grow along the forest floor. Wild flowers such as fireweed, tundra rose, lady's slipper, milk vetch, and Labrador tea add a touch of color.

A high brush zone of birch, alder, and willow thickets occurs at tree line, creating a transitional environment between forests and alpine tundra.

Alpine tundra appears as mountain meadows

(Left ←) Sedge tussocks and spruce trees make difficult terrain for hikers along the Ernie Creek Valley.
(Jon Nickles)

(Below ↓) This dwarf fireweed pokes out from a sand bar along the Middle Fork Koyukuk.
(Bill Sherwonit)

Scattered spruce and deciduous trees along the creek bottom mark the northern tree line through the Endicott Mountains. (Jon Nickles)

Colorful ground cover, including sphagnum moss, lowbush cranberries, blueberries, bearberries, and mountain heather, is prevalent throughout alpine tundra surrounding the Koyukuk River Valley.
(Shelley Schneider)

17

generally at elevations of 2,000 to 4,000 feet. Vegetation is sparse, and plants usually reach no more than a few inches in height. This community includes lichens, blueberries, crowberries, stunted arctic poppies, paintbrushes, monkshoods, moss campions, and bluebells.

Most terrain within the Koyukuk drainage is bare of vegetation above 4,500 feet.

Within and south of the Brooks Range, patches of moist tundra grow in the lowlands. This tundra contains a wide variety of low-growing shrubs, grasses, and wild flowers within a mat of lichens and mosses. Moist tundra is home of sedge tussocks, clumps of grasses that widen as they grow upward forming top-heavy, mushroom-shaped masses.

Fauna

If the lion is king of the jungle, then the grizzly is lord of the Arctic. Grizzly bears are generally solitary; however, they do not have territories as such. Their ranges may overlap that of several other bears.

Because of the marginal conditions in which they live, the grizzly population of the Arctic is small. In the mountainous terrain of the upper Koyukuk region, for example, there may be only one bear per 50 to 100 square miles.

Grizzlies emerge from their dens in April and return to their lairs in October. During the short northern summer, bears are very mobile; male grizzlies may have ranges of up to 900 square miles. Ranges of females, especially those with cubs, are much smaller, but they too may roam over areas as large as 100 square miles. But most grizzlies do have a home area used for denning, breeding, and most foraging. The brown monarchs can be found roaming tundra lowlands, spruce forests, river valleys, and steep mountain slopes.

Grizzlies are omnivorous; their diet ranges from grasses, sedges, roots, and berries, to other animals

(Opposite ←) Autumn colors brighten this tranquil scene along Bonanza Creek, a good stream for grayling fishing, whose waters eventually join those of the South Fork Koyukuk. (Steve McCutcheon)

(Below ↓) Marginal habitat forces the grizzly population of the upper Koyukuk to spread out in search of food. In some areas the habitat may support only one bear per 50 to 100 square miles. (Steve McCutcheon)

such as small mammals, caribou, moose, and occasionally even other bears.

Black bears also roam Koyukuk country, but they prefer the forested valleys. They will, however, cross alpine tundra in search of berries and roots.

Unlike the grizzly and black bear, which tend to be solitary, the Koyukuk drainage is also home to a mammal which prefers the company of thousands, the caribou.

The western arctic caribou herd winters in Koyukuk country. Each spring these ungulates migrate north of the Brooks Range to feed and bear their young on the arctic plain. In August, they begin their yearly trek south along traditional routes through the central Brooks Range such as Anaktuvuk Pass until settling in the southern Brooks Range or in foothills and lowlands to the south. There they feed on lichens and grasses on hillside slopes or along lakes and rivers. In the spring they again begin their long march north.

Caribou, like other herd animals, undergo cycles in their population. In the early 1970s, the western arctic herd numbered about 240,000. By 1975, however, the herd had shrunk to less than 100,000. Since then herd size has been increasing and by early 1983 had reached 175,000.

Koyukuk country is home to other large mammals, particularly Dall sheep and moose. The only wild white sheep in the world, Dall sheep live in small, scattered bands within the Brooks Range. Although they may feed along streams in valley bottoms, they spend most of their time along mountain ridges, often on steep slopes that seem all

A herd of caribou takes off across a sand bar. Among the favored game of the Koyukuk, caribou migrate through mountain passes in the Brooks Range from their calving grounds on the arctic plain to wintering grounds on the south side of the range.
(Steve McCutcheon)

but impossible to negotiate. The sheep stay in the mountains even during the coldest months of winter, inhabiting slopes blown clear of snow where they can find forage.

Moose, like that precious metal gold, are wherever you find them. And that can be just about anywhere within the Koyukuk region, from marshes of the broad lowlands to alpine meadows at elevations of 4,000 feet or more. Most commonly, however, moose frequent broad valleys within the spruce-hardwood forests, muskeg bogs, and river bars where they can browse on young willow shoots.

A chief predator of the Koyukuk region is the wolf which, like the moose, inhabits a wide range of environments but prefers forested valleys. This legendary carnivore feeds on a wide variety of animals from small rodents to caribou and moose.

The Koyukuk drainage supports a number of small mammals species — wolverines, snowshoe hares, porcupines, red foxes, martens, lynx, squirrels, marmots, mink, weasels, shrews, and mice — all of which fill their niche in the food chain and some of which provide the pelts and meat prized by the region's year-round human residents.

The Koyukuk shelters an abundant variety of bird species, from loons and other waterfowl that take advantage of the many lakes and ponds, to game birds such as ptarmigan and grouse; from raptors like eagles, hawks, and owls, to the smaller passerine, or perching, birds. A few hardy species — jays, ravens, chickadees, and grosbeaks, for example — remain year-round.

Completeing the wildlife picture of Koyukuk country are the salmon, trout, arctic grayling, arctic char, northern pike, lingcod, and whitefish that inhabit the region's lakes and streams. The Koyukuk and its tributaries are closed to commercial fishing, but salmon, and later in the season, whitefish, add substantially to the subsistence diet of the region's Eskimo and Athabascan inhabitants.

Alaska has numerous species of small rodents: voles, mice, and lemmings, which range throughout the state. These youngsters, blind and calling to one another, were found at the base of a spruce tree in the upper Koyukuk drainage.
(Penny Rennick)

Red foxes roam throughout Koyukuk country where the cold, dry climate seems to produce a higher quality fur than do warmer climates to the south.
(Steve McCutcheon)

Largest of traditional game animals in the Koyukuk, moose prefer lowland forests, bogs, and river bars but they can be found in other habitat.
(Steve McCutcheon)

(Left ←) *Normally considered birds of the sea, some species of gulls nest and feed far inland. This Bonaparte's gull nests in low conifers and breeds in lowland forests near lakes and ponds, typical habitat in the Koyukuk River Valley.*
(Steve McCutcheon)

(Below ↓) *An arctic loon takes off from the Alatna River, which winds its way for 145 miles through the Endicott Mountains to meet with the Koyukuk at Allakaket.* (Shelley Schneider)

(Above ↕) *One of the tastiest fish of the Koyukuk drainage is the arctic grayling, distinguished by its large dorsal fin. Grayling range across the continent from the western shore of Canada's Hudson Bay to the west coast of Alaska.* (John and Margaret Ibbotson)

(Right →) *A fisherman tries his luck at Ernie Lake, a frequent destination for visitors to the North Fork Koyukuk River Valley. The lake was named for Ernie Johnson, an early-day miner and trapper who explored the Koyukuk wilderness.*
(George Wuerthner)

(Above ♦) *Two cultures share the Koyukuk on its 550-mile run up from the Yukon River. The upper Koyukuk is Eskimo country, whereas the lower river is homeland of the Athabascan Indians of Alaska's Interior. Following primarily a subsistence lifestyle, the Athabascans have gathered at four villages on the lower Koyukuk: Allakaket, Hughes, Huslia (shown here), and Koyukuk, at the river's mouth.* (Penny Rennick, staff)

(Left ←) *A visitor measures water temperatures at Kanuti Hot Springs, just outside the boundary of Kanuti National Wildlife Refuge in the lowlands of the lower Koyukuk. Hot springs temperatures in this area measure about 120° as heated water leaks from geothermal reservoirs deep within the earth.* (Gil Mull)

Early Explorers and Prospectors on the Koyukuk

By Terrence Cole
Editor, The ALASKA JOURNAL®

Editor's note: *Many of the historical photos in this issue are credited to Jasper Wyman, a native of Illinois and a rancher by trade, who joined the Galesburg-Alaska Mining and Development Company for the trek to the Koyukuk in 1898. Wyman's hobby was photography, and he sold copies of his photos of the gold rush to help finance his unsuccessful mining venture in the north.*

The Koyukuk River and its tributaries drain the south side of the central Brooks Range, one of the last great mountain systems in North America to be mapped and explored. Not until the twentieth century was the true size and extent of the 600-mile-long mountain range known, and it is still today one of the most rugged wilderness areas in the world.

The upper Koyukuk is one of the oldest and most isolated mining districts in Alaska. About 100 years ago the first prospectors came to this remote valley to search for gold. They followed the footsteps of Lt. Henry T. Allen, a 26-year-old army officer who made the first exploration of the Koyukuk River in 1885. Before that time almost nothing was known about the upper Koyukuk. A few explorers and traders had traveled on the lower reaches of the river, but the upper Koyukuk, as Allen put it, was "terra incognita."

In about five months in 1885, Allen mapped and explored a vast portion of interior Alaska for the first time. He ascended the Copper River in March 1885, and descended the Tanana River to the Yukon, a journey which by itself would have been remarkable. No explorer had ever crossed the Alaska Range to the Yukon before, and neither the Copper nor the Tanana rivers had been previously explored. Though he had not been ordered to explore the Koyukuk, Allen was eager to continue his expedition and to map a third little-known river in Alaska. Accompanied by Pvt. Fred Fickett and several Indian packers, Allen followed an overland trail north from the Yukon on the divide between the Melozitna and the Tozitna rivers, and battling swarms of sand flies and mosquitoes, he descended the Kanuti River to the Koyukuk.

Lieutenant Allen's map of the Koyukuk Valley shows the river twisting through more than 500 miles of unexplored territory. He ascended the

In 1885 Lt. Henry T. Allen made a remarkable 1,500-mile journey, mapping and exploring a large portion of interior Alaska. Allen's travels included the first exploration of the upper Koyukuk River. (University of Alaska, Anchorage)

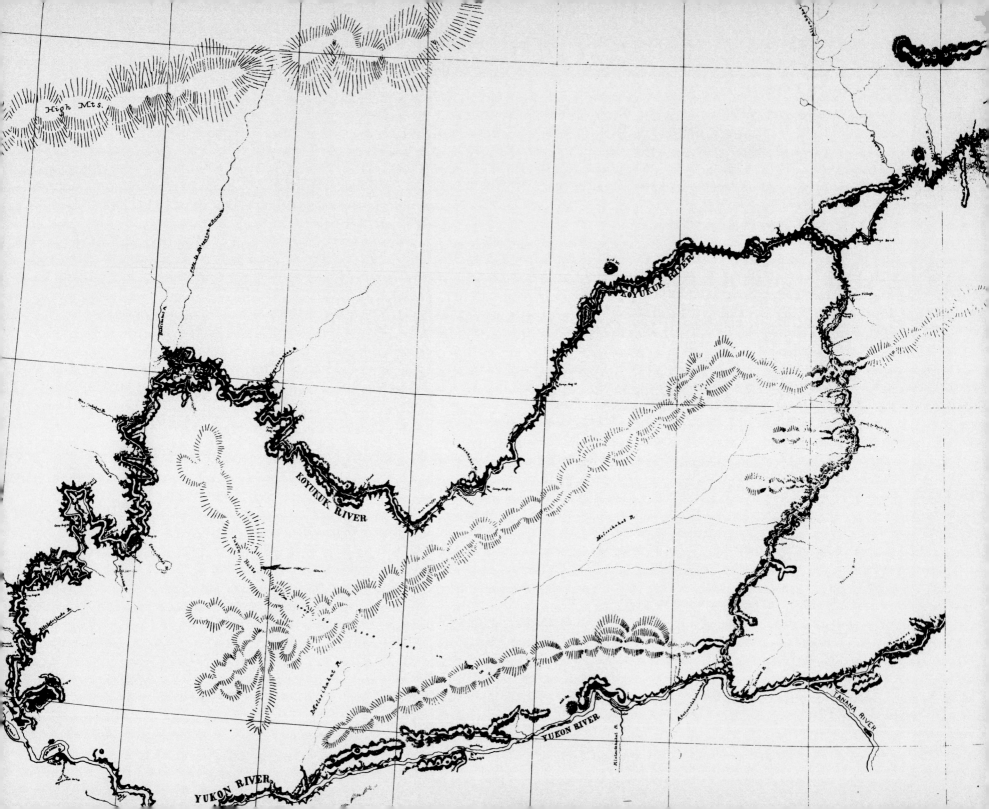

Koyukuk to a short distance upstream from the present-day community of Bettles Field, known generally as Bettles, to a tributary he called the "Fickett River," before he ran low on supplies and had to turn back.

"We were beyond the habitations of the natives," Allen wrote, "in a country of little game, with about eight pounds of rice and beans, ten pounds of flour, three pounds of bacon, and two pounds of lard." The source of the "Fickett River" was somewhere in the range of "High Mountains" which Allen sketched in across the top of the map, but he could not proceed any farther.

In the late 1880s, half a dozen prospectors followed Henry Allen into the unknown country of the upper Koyukuk, and miners have been digging for gold in the region ever since. One of the first prospectors in the Koyukuk was John Bremner, who had traveled on the Copper and Tanana rivers with Lieutenant Allen, but had remained on the Yukon during his exploration of the Koyukuk. Bremner prospected for gold on the Koyukuk in 1886 and 1887, but was murdered by an Indian on the Hogatza River in about 1888. One of the last streams Bremner had prospected was Henry Allen's "Fickett River," and in Bremner's memory his friends called it "Old John's River," or the John River as it is known today.

There are many versions of the story, but when the miners on the Yukon learned of Bremner's murder, they vowed to seek revenge. About two dozen men formed a posse to find the murderers and to punish them. One of the ringleaders of the

In 1885, Lt. Henry T. Allen made the first reconnaisance of the Koyukuk River, mapping more than 500 miles of previously unexplored territory. Off to the north on this portion of Allen's map is the range of "High Mountains" which he saw, now known as the Brooks Range. (From Military Reconnoissance in Alaska [sic], by Henry T. Allen)

vigilantes was Gordon C. Bettles, a 29-year-old miner and trader for whom the town of Bettles on the Koyukuk was later named. In July 1888 the miners' posse commandeered one of the small trading steamers which operated on the Yukon, and headed up the Koyukuk under a full head of steam. Within a few days they reached an Indian camp and found a cache filled with Bremner's tools. The miners captured a young Indian about 20 years old who allegedly admitted to having killed Bremner, and on the return trip to the Yukon the posse found him guilty.

"There was a big tree bending over the river," one of the miners recalled many years later. "We made a noose, tried it and it worked too slow, that is didn't slip so well, so Hank sent me for axle grease or lard to grease the rope and it worked fine. We again put it on the Indian and everybody pulled on the rope and tied him up and started for home." The vigilantes fired several shots into the young Indian's body, and as a warning to others, left him hanging from the tree, near the mouth of the Koyukuk River.

After Bremner's death a few prospectors continued to explore the creeks in the Koyukuk Valley. During the 1890s several miners discovered gold in the bars of the river where the diggings were easy, such as Hughes Bar and Tramway Bar, but large numbers of gold seekers only arrived in the Koyukuk with the Klondike gold rush of 1898.

When gold was discovered in the Klondike in Canada in the late 1890s, tens of thousands of people landed in Alaska, determined to become rich, even if it took them all summer. In the wild excitement of the stampede, rumors about new discoveries spread like a contagious disease. Usually the farther away the new gold field was, the richer it was supposed to be, and because the Koyukuk was far away from everywhere, more than 1,000 inexperienced gold hunters rushed into the valley in 1898. For one summer at least, about 50 steamboats jammed the river like never before

and never since, carrying the stampeders upstream into the foothills of the Brooks Range.

Wherever they landed, the mining companies founded their own "towns" in which to spend the winter. Seventy-five miles up the Alatna River, a mining company from Beaver, Pennsylvania, christened their camp Beaver City, though West Beaver was already located nearby. Along the South and Middle forks of the Koyukuk there were more than half a dozen other places in 1898, with names such as Arctic City, New Arctic City, Bergman, Peavy, Union City, Seaforth, Soo City, and Jimtown. These "cities" were mostly clearings in the woods along the riverbank, with a few shacks, a sawmill, and a steamboat. Almost all of them were abandoned in less than a year, but a few were more substantial.

Peavy had its own schoolhouse, and a blueprint of the townsite mapped out the broad streets and avenues which would supposedly someday be blazed through the spruce trees. Arctic City had electric lights, which glistened through the darkness during the long arctic winter of 1898-99, and a large dance hall. However, the town of Bergman was more famous for its night life.

"This town, for its size," a Koyukuk stampeder wrote of Bergman in the winter of 1898-99, "was one of the toughest I had ever seen at that time, and

Koyukuk pioneer Gordon C. Bettles, second row, extreme left, poses in 1894 with other members of the Yukon Order of Pioneers. Bettles came to Alaska in 1885, landing at Juneau and continuing on over the Chilkoot Pass to the Yukon River Valley, where he was one of the first white residents. In 1894 he became editor and publisher of the Yukon Press. *He then moved north, and between 1898 and 1900 he and partners Frank and Charles Pickarts established trading posts at Bergman, Coldfoot, and Bettles.* (Charles Bunnell Collection, University of Alaska, Fairbanks, Archives)

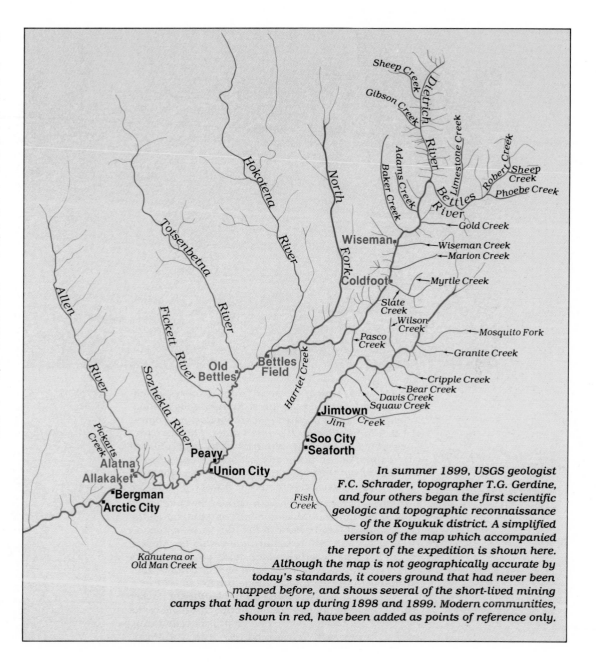

In summer 1899, USGS geologist F.C. Schrader, topographer T.G. Gerdine, and four others began the first scientific geologic and topographic reconnaissance of the Koyukuk district. A simplified version of the map which accompanied the report of the expedition is shown here. Although the map is not geographically accurate by today's standards, it covers ground that had never been mapped before, and shows several of the short-lived mining camps that had grown up during 1898 and 1899. Modern communities, shown in red, have been added as points of reference only.

(Above ↑) *One of the small mining towns which sprang up along the upper Koyukuk was Peavy, which in 1899 boasted a schoolhouse, post office, U.S. land office, and a small store. The store was operated by Mr. W.H. Windrick, who kept a liberal supply of canned goods; all other staples had to come from the supply post at Bergman, about 50 river miles downstream.* (F.C. Schrader, 437, USGS)

(Right →) *Twenty-three members of the Galesburg-Alaska Mining and Development Company sit on the steps at Leschi Park in Seattle, Washington, on May 2, 1898, before departing by ship for Alaska. The expedition was made up of men from Galesburg, Illinois, who hoped to make their fortunes in the gold fields along the Koyukuk River. They were accompanied by photographer Jasper Wyman, whose photographic chronicle of the venture exists today.*
(Jasper Wyman; courtesy of Jean M. Moore)

2nd Round
Bergman. Alaska.
Mar:31–1899

Prize fighters Jack Kelly of Denver, Colorado, and J.C. Cox of Los Angeles, California, battle during the second round of their challenge on March 31, 1899, at the mining camp of Bergman. Kelly bested his opponent in five rounds and won the $150 prize; Cox took away $50 for his efforts. (Jasper Wyman; courtesy of Jean M. Moore)

the amount of whiskey those two or three hundred people would get away with in a day was astonishing. Their favorite amusements, after they had become pretty full, were fighting and wrestling, shooting out the lights, and also shooting the cabin full of holes." Bergman also had more organized entertainment. In March 1899, in an outdoor ring, Ed Kelly knocked out J.C. Cox in a five-round boxing match. The Cox-Kelly contest was a "hot fight from start to finish," and was reportedly the "first scientific prize fight ever fought in Alaska north of the Arctic Circle."

Probably 90 percent of the stampeders left the Koyukuk in 1899 bitterly disappointed. As one man who had wintered in Beaver City wrote, "After I left the old shack I never turned back to take a last look, for there was nothing to see or remember about it but suffering." Few of the stampeders had done any prospecting, and many of the poorly prepared newcomers had scurvy. They vowed never to spend another winter in the Arctic again, and left as soon as the ice broke up on the Koyukuk in the spring of 1899, leaving behind a half-dozen ghost towns in the Koyukuk Valley, marked only by a few rotting cabins and wrecked steamboats.

About 100 prospectors may have remained behind in the Koyukuk after the 1898 stampede, and these men did the real work of developing the mines in the region. The first major gold discovery was made on Myrtle Creek in the spring of 1899, and the town of Coldfoot sprang up nearby. In the following years prospectors struck gold on nearly

(Above ↕) *Miners crowd together for a group photo in front of Pickarts, Bettles, & Pickarts store at Bergman on April 27, 1899. Bergman was located on the Koyukuk River, about eight miles southeast of the present village of Allakaket.*
(Jasper Wyman; courtesy of Jean M. Moore)

(Below ↕) *Dressed in their finest, members of the Bergman String Band pose in front of a cabin in this photo taken April 2, 1899.* (Jasper Wyman; courtesy of Jean M. Moore)

every major stream in the region. By far the richest discovery was made in the diggings on Nolan Creek in about 1906, a stream which produced more than $800,000 in gold during the next four or five years.

Not far from the Nolan Creek diggings, at the mouth of Wiseman Creek, a town sprang up in about 1909 which was first called Wright City and Nolan. Later the name was changed to Wiseman (and another mining camp a few miles up Wiseman Creek took on the name Nolan). Coldfoot was soon abandoned, and Wiseman became the metropolis of the upper Koyukuk, a community which has survived to the present day.

The Koyukuk mining district was one of the most isolated in Alaska, and from 1900 to 1930 total gold production of the region was only about $5 million. The high cost of transportation to the Koyukuk made it one of the most expensive mining camps in the world. The center of light-draft steamboat navigation on the Koyukuk was Bettles, a trading post and townsite staked by Gordon C. Bettles in 1900, about one mile below the mouth of the John River. The gold fields, however, were another 75 miles above Bettles, and every pound of freight and supplies for the Koyukuk had to be hauled the rest of the way by poling boats or horse-drawn scows.

It was the extreme isolation of Alaska's most northern mining camp which made the Koyukuk unique, and early observers often commented that the Koyukuk was the friendliest place in Alaska.

"The remoteness and difficulty of the Koyukuk camp," Archdeacon Hudson Stuck wrote in about 1917, "have engendered a feeling of comradeship amongst the miners that is not found, I think, in any other camp." Yet a friendly spirit was not the only distinguishing trait of life in the Koyukuk. Stuck had to admit that there was probably more whiskey consumed per capita in the Koyukuk than anywhere in the world, a distinction worthy of the mining camp where the first scientific prize fight in the Alaska Arctic had been staged.

Members of the Galesburg-Alaska Mining and Development Company, with 13 sleds and two dog teams, take to the trail on March 23, 1899, outside Beaver City, on the Alatna River at the mouth of Helpmejack Creek. The group's efforts to strike it rich were a failure; in June 1899, just one year after their arrival, the men set out on the Yukon River, beginning the first leg of their long journey home.
(Jasper Wyman; courtesy of Jean M. Moore)

(Left ←) *Two miners try their luck on Myrtle Creek in 1899. The bank of the creek is lined with slaty schist, a crystalline rock which tends to split into thin slabs, in which gold occurs.*
(F.C. Schrader, 402, USGS)

(Right →) *The first major gold discovery on the upper Koyukuk was made on Myrtle Creek by Knute Ellingson in spring of 1899. This photo, taken during the summer of that year, shows Ellingson and two helpers at their sluicing operation.*
(F.C. Schrader, 406, USGS)

The steamer Ben Hur of Nome *pulls up to the riverbank at Hughes on June 29, 1911. The village was established in 1910 as a supply center for the nearby Indian River gold placers.*
(P.S. Smith, 750, USGS)

BEN HUR OF NOME.

One of the problems encountered by early-day miners on the upper Koyukuk was the difficulty in getting supplies up the shallow river. Steamboats could go as far as Bettles, where freight was transferred to horse-drawn scows for the trip to Coldfoot or Wiseman. This photo was taken in 1919 near Coldfoot. (A.G. Maddren, 19, USGS)

Tishu's World

By Tishu Ulen, as told to Shirley English

Editor's note: *Shirley English, teacher and musician, has long been familiar with the Koyukuk region and with Tishu's world. While in college, she met William English, Jr., Tishu's half brother; later she and Bill English were married. Tishu turned to Shirley when she decided to record her memories of Koyukuk country, and we are grateful to Shirley for sharing* Tishu's World *with ALASKA GEOGRAPHIC® readers.*

In the context of this article, William English, Sr., is the husband of Mrs. Mary English, and William English, Jr., is their son. The senior Mr. English has since passed away, and William English, Jr., now has a son, also named William English, Jr. The third generation Mr. English does not appear in this account.

Introduction

In Alaska's Interior is a wilderness known as the upper Koyukuk, where darkness and cold reign for seven months of the year, and where summers are short interludes between breakup and freezeup. Here, in a valley beside the Middle Fork of the Koyukuk River and sheltered by peaks of the Brooks Range, nestles the village of Wiseman. Here too, in the isolation of 200 miles north of Fairbanks, developed a community of Eskimos and whites who comprised the world of Tishu Ulen. Together they shared a rigorous but enjoyable frontier life.

To appreciate Tishu's world, one must know something of this land she calls home. The gold strikes in Koyukuk country were never as celebrated as other mineral rushes to the territory of Alaska. Perhaps the distances between and number of creeks involved in the Koyukuk discoveries provided less drama when compared to other gold rushes, or perhaps the region lacked a Jack London or Rex Beach to immortalize some of the colorful characters who spent a portion of their lives there.

At the time of the Klondike gold rush to Yukon Territory in the 1890s, the upper Koyukuk was inhabited by only a few Kobuk and Nunamiut

Prospectors work their claim along Helpmejack Creek which flows into the Alatna River 66 miles northeast of Hughes. In winter, miners built fires to thaw the ground, then dug out the dirt and piled it where it could be sluiced in spring and summer. As the hole deepened, they constructed a windlass over the opening to raise and lower workers and to raise buckets of dirt. These workers have dug their hole to a depth of 51 feet. Water filling in the holes prevented miners from digging in the summer; consequently, the digging took place in winter and the sluicing in spring and summer when water was plentiful. (Jasper Wyman; courtesy of Jean M. Moore)

Prospecting Hole on Hello Me Jackal
Jan 5 - 1899 - ...th 5ft.

Eskimos, whose living depended largely on caribou. An overflow of gold seekers from the Klondike brought the first miners into Koyukuk country in fall 1898. Most of the miners departed the following spring, but not before they had prospected and named the creeks that showed traces of gold.

As the promise of gold was realized at Slate, Myrtle, and Emma creeks, the Northern Commercial Company and William Plummer opened stores

Residents of Arctic City, a mining camp near where the Kanuti River enters the Koyukuk, pause to have their photo taken on August 21, 1898. Although few white women came into Koyukuk country in the early days, some wives did accompany their husbands in the search for gold. (Jasper Wyman; courtesy of Jean M. Moore)

at Coldfoot, some 70 river miles upstream from Bettles and named because a group of stampeders got cold feet at this point and turned back. Coldfoot had its heyday and declined almost as quickly as it had mushroomed, for the new strike at Nolan Creek shifted population upstream again, this time to near Wright's Roadhouse on bubbling Wiseman Creek. The community which grew up here was first named Nolan and later Wiseman in honor of an obscure prospector who panned the creek and moved on, leaving only his name behind.

Wiseman flourished as a hub of mining activity. When Verne Watts found the riches of the Hammond River in 1911, the prosperity of Wiseman was assured for a time. Hundreds of miners and business people came and went. In Wiseman they bought supplies and enjoyed a lively social life. Gold production became more sophisticated on the creeks, and various types of sluicing and drifting continued until World War II. As the price of gold lagged further and further behind the cost of producing it, Koyukuk activity slowed to a snail's pace. Most miners retired to outside Alaska or to population centers within the territory. A few old-timers lingered on with their memories.

But the only certainty in life is change, and changes have come to all of Alaska. In the early days, rivers were the summer and winter highways of the Interior. When Noel Wien landed his Hisso Standard on the river bar at Wiseman in spring 1925, a new age had begun. The airplane, along with radio communication, ended the isolation of arctic Alaska. Dog teams and horse-drawn barges were no longer indispensable in moving people and supplies. Bettles Field, a new community, grew up around an airport, located a few miles upstream from Old Bettles. Then came construction of the pipeline haul road, now designated the Dalton Highway, in the 1970s. Coldfoot, a ghost town, was reborn as a truck stop. And Wiseman, diminished to a handful of year-round residents, slowly has

(Left ←) *Steamboats carried passengers up the Koyukuk to the head of navigation at Bettles. Sometimes currents and shifting sand bars caused the boats to run aground. Here the steamer* Illinois *pulls the* Jennie M *off a gravel bar near the junction of the Alatna and Koyukuk rivers. (Allenkaket is an earlier name for the Alatna River.)*
(Jasper Wyman; courtesy of Jean M. Moore)

(Below ↓) *Most residents of the upper Koyukuk got their supplies by river. From Bettles, shallow scows, such as this one belonging to Sam Dubin, carried freight to Wiseman, Coldfoot, and other upstream localities.*
(Courtesy of Tishu Ulen)

revived as a recreation and guide headquarters for hunters. Even the main channel of the Koyukuk that used to flow in front of the log trading post has now moved a quarter of a mile away. Only the mountains remain unchanged as the midnight sun in June dips behind them, leaving a magic glow in the evening sky.

The life of Tishu is woven into the Koyukuk. Here is her account of life the past 100 years in this part of Alaska as seen through her eyes and those of her mother, Mrs. Mary English. Larger historical events are viewed only as they impacted the life of the closely knit and interdependent society in which Tishu moved.

— Shirley English

Koyukuk on Yukon R
Aug 8 1898
J. N. Wyman Ht
Galesburg Ill

(Above ↑) *First stop on the long push up the Koyukuk River is the village of Koyukuk at the mouth of the river where it joins the Yukon. Three men (center) wear mosquito netting to ward off the insects which plague travel in Alaska's Interior in summer.* (Jasper Wyman; courtesy of Jean M. Moore)

(Right →) *Wood was the all-purpose fuel during early days along the Koyukuk, firing boilers of steamboats, generating heat for miners' cabins, and sustaining fires for thawing ground at the miners' diggings. Here members of the Galesburg-Alaska Mining and Development Company cut wood along the Koyukuk River on August 11, 1898.* (Jasper Wyman; courtesy of Jean M. Moore)

The photographer's inscription on this photo reads "Rapid City, Alaska, Dec. 21, 1898, 60° below 0." The "city" reportedly consisted of four cabins and several tents hastily built in the autumn of 1898 when a group of miners was caught by an early freezeup on the Alatna River. It was apparently occupied only one winter. (Jasper Wyman, courtesy of Jean M. Moore)

H. Hall, Ed Bergson (on top), and an unidentified helper whipsaw lumber at a mining camp at West Beaver, on the Alatna River, October 14, 1898. (Jasper Wyman, courtesy of Gary Ingman)

J.J. Ewing, his face showing signs of the hardships endured by miners on the Koyukuk, sits in his tent at Bergman on April 27, 1899. (Jasper Wyman, courtesy of Jean M. Moore)

George Gold, John Bradshaw, and Harry Parsons pull their sled through Hells Gate on Rockybottom Creek in January 1899. (Jasper Wyman, courtesy of Jean M. Moore)

Two mail carriers, identified as Bunger and Beaton, make their way down the frozen Koyukuk River in April 1899. (Jasper Wyman, courtesy of Gary Ingman)

Not all life in Koyukuk country at the turn of the century was digging in the mud or chopping wood. These ladies enjoy a tea party at the Bettles cabin at Bergman on April 7, 1899. (Jasper Wyman; courtesy of Jean M. Moore)

This trio of miners passes a long evening playing cards at a cabin on Beaver Creek, west of the Alatna River, in January 1899. (Jasper Wyman; courtesy of Jean M. Moore)

Earliest Memories

My name is Tishu Ulen, and my people are Inupiat Eskimos from Kobuk River country. [The Kobuk River is the major drainage to the west of the Koyukuk. The Kobuk flows more than 300 miles to enter Hotham Inlet, an arm of the Chukchi Sea, near Kotzebue. — Ed.] I was born in May 1905 in a tent at the lower end of Big Chandalar Lake in the Brooks Range. Nakuchluk, wife of my mother's uncle, helped bring me into the world. My father was a good Eskimo hunter who had to travel through much of the country to find game. My mother and father had traveled most of their lives — by dog team in winter and by river boat in summer — from the western coast of Alaska as far east as the Christian River, and as far north as Barrow. They seldom went south of the Koyukuk River. That was Indian country.

When I was just a baby I became very sick. My parents had already lost three children before me, and they were worried. They took me to Dr. Brooks at the new gold camp of Nolan. He saved my life. For a month he and his wife kept me at their cabin, and my father paid for my care by bringing fresh meat. Mrs. Brooks insisted that she didn't want gold dust. Instead she wanted five moose livers, six hearts, and two hams in payment. After I got well, we didn't travel much anymore. My father still went hunting, but my mother didn't follow him. Constant traveling was a hard life for everyone.

I spent most of my life in and around Wiseman, a gold camp on the Middle Fork of the Koyukuk. My first memory is of walking with my mother in the moonlight and really noticing the beautiful mountains around us. I never forgot that night, and I always look up at those mountains. Every day they are different. They are a part of my life.

My next memory is when my mother took me over to Kobuk country with my uncle Isaac and cousin Pingalo. We started in April from Bettles, went down the river ice by dog team to Alatna, up the Alatna River, and then crossed over to the Kobuk River. The portage took about a week. We spent our spring at Long Beach, now called Shungnak. Then with other friends and relatives we floated down the Kobuk River on poling boats to Kotzebue. Everyone took turns rowing. We slept by day in different villages along the way and traveled by night, because it was cool and there were no mosquitoes. We kept our dogs with us in the boats for the trip back upriver. I remember waking up in the morning and hearing singing. Those in the first boat started the day with a hymn, in the next boat they sang Eskimo dance songs, and in the last boat they sang Eskimo love songs. You don't hear Eskimo love songs anymore. The singing was beautiful, and I will remember those happy days always.

On that trip we traded furs at Kotzebue with Alaskan and Siberian Eskimos as well as with white people. The camps spread out for miles along the beach. We did a lot of visiting and dancing. After a month of trading, we started back to Shungnak by boat, pulled by our dogs running along the bank. We had no motors in those days. A few of our people stayed in the Kobuk, but the rest started back toward the Koyukuk in the fall. After freezeup, we left by dog team for the mouth of the Alatna River and the villages of Alatna and Allakaket.

Saint John's-in-the-Wilderness is the Episcopal mission there that served the Indians on the south side of the river and the Eskimos on the north side. The people from both villages got along well together. They visited back and forth across the river and attended services at Saint John's. The older people could even speak one another's language. Here I saw my first Christmas celebration, a big potlatch which lasted 10 days. They held a big dance too, and I saw my first square dance. I thought it was funny the way everybody jerked each other every which way.

*A group stops for lunch at Windy Arm, on the trail
between Coldfoot and Bettles in about 1917.
Identified in the photo are, from left: Susie McNeal
with three of her children; Harry Snowden, an
Eskimo from Kobuk; unidentified girl in fur parka;
Tishu Ulen; Mary English; and Captain Haines,
possibly the same man who was captain of the river
boat* Koyukuk *during the early 1900s.*
(Courtesy of William English, Jr.)

A single log cabin served as store and post office at the village of Koyukuk in August 1898. The village, located at the confluence of the Yukon and Koyukuk rivers, was a supply point for river boats carrying prospectors to the gold fields upstream.
(Jasper Wyman, courtesy of Gary Ingman)

In the spring we went up the Koyukuk River to Bettles. There was much excitement when the first river boat came into Bettles in June. A scow had come downstream from Wiseman in late May to meet the steamer in Bettles, since the steamboats couldn't get any farther upstream. The scow had big sweepers on each end so it could be pulled by horses across the shallow parts of the river. The steamboats burned wood for power, and we passed several woodcutting camps along the way.

I remember standing on the bank at Bettles watching the scow from Wiseman being unloaded. Several men used wooden poles that bent under the weight of small wooden boxes. I didn't know at the time that gold was so heavy. The gold in the upper Koyukuk came mostly from underground mining that they called "drifting." An inch-wide, 100-foot rope was spliced around each box of gold in case

the scow swamped on the river. From Bettles the boxes were sent Outside on the steamboat *Reliance*, or sometimes the *Nina*, the *James Dietrich*, or the *Rock Island*.

A lot of people were traveling up and down the Koyukuk River in those days. I remember that Volney Richmond of Northern Commercial Company was always the first passenger off the boat at Bettles in the spring. He always carried a stack of books under his arm. Then would begin the unloading of freight, and I stood waiting with excitement for the cases of oranges, apples, and lemons to be delivered to the store. I couldn't wait to taste fruit after the long winter. I remember once having three whole dollars of my own money for fruit. I ate everything, peelings and all. In those days, a Sunday treat was a slice of bacon. The few eggs we tasted were many months old and pretty

This photo, taken about 1914, shows some of the sourdoughs at Carl Frank's roadhouse opposite Tramway Bar. On the Middle Fork Koyukuk River about 24 miles southwest of Wiseman, Tramway Bar is the site of a gold discovery as early as 1893.
(Courtesy of Tishu Ulen)

strong. I never did care for the powdered milk they called Klim.

I didn't have much in the way of toys in those days. Wherever we were I played caribou bone games, sailed little boats, played store with rocks and mud in cans, went sliding on the ice or sledding behind a dog. I was always outdoors, winter and summer. I fished, picked berries, and even started trapping weasels when I was about nine because I wanted to earn money for cloth for a real dress.

Mama and other Eskimo women would pick big buckets of blueberries to sell at the scows and steamers the day they landed. They got about a dollar a gallon for berries. And then they would fish for whitefish, king salmon, and dog salmon to sell to the miners who were hungry for fresh fish. I recall an old couple who couldn't speak English brought in a big king that they had netted in an eddy above Bettles. The miners rushed over and cut slices from the salmon until all that was left was a head and tail. Of course they paid for the fish, but no one understood that the old couple really wanted the fish for themselves. They were angry.

One time Mama caught two whitefish. We took

Okpik along and gave her one fish to cook. Sammy Hope gave Mama a dollar for the other fish. Then along came a miner with a knife, chopped the fish in half, and gave Mama two more dollars. Mama never said a word. White people did funny things.

When we traveled in winter, we used a tent with a small stove. The dogs were staked outside. Mama cooked with a big, black frying pan. Our main food was fish, caribou, or moose meat, but sometimes we'd have Alaska potatoes (roots) with fish oil and berries. Mama gathered robin eggs in the spring and baked them in the campfire. Sometimes we gathered willow shoots in early spring, when we always craved fresh food. The shoots were juicy from the sap and a little like lettuce. After dinner I'd snuggle down to sleep under a rabbit skin blanket lined with flannel that Mama made. Underneath were more warm skins.

After my mother and father separated when I was young, Mama supported us by fur sewing. She could make almost anything. I missed my father for years. When I finally saw him again, I told him I'd been waiting for him for a long time. After I was married, my father came to Wiseman and visited me. He brought moose and sheep meat. He was always a good hunter and provider.

I remember well Jack White's scow at Bettles. Jessie Hastings and I used to watch the loading from the bank of the river. One day while fishing upstream, Jessie and I saw smoke. We ran to the scow and saw that the horse blankets were on fire and no one was around. They were awfully heavy, but Jessie and I managed to pull them out and dump them in the river. When Jack showed up, we told him what we'd done. He was pleased because we'd saved his scow. He told us, "When you get married, I'm going to buy you a wedding present." At that time we didn't even know what a wedding present was. But he never forgot. Jessie died young, but when I got married, Jack brought me a big double bed. After all those years he had remembered.

(Above ↑) *The upper Koyukuk had its share of saloons during the heyday of the gold rush, and gold nuggets were welcome as payment for services. Jack Nelson, a saloonkeeper in Wiseman, holds some of the gold brought in by his patrons.* (Courtesy of Tishu Ulen)

(Right →) *The first detailed map of the upper Koyukuk River was compiled in 1932 from U.S. Geological Survey maps and firsthand reconnaissance by forester Robert Marshall.* (USGS Bulletin #844-E)

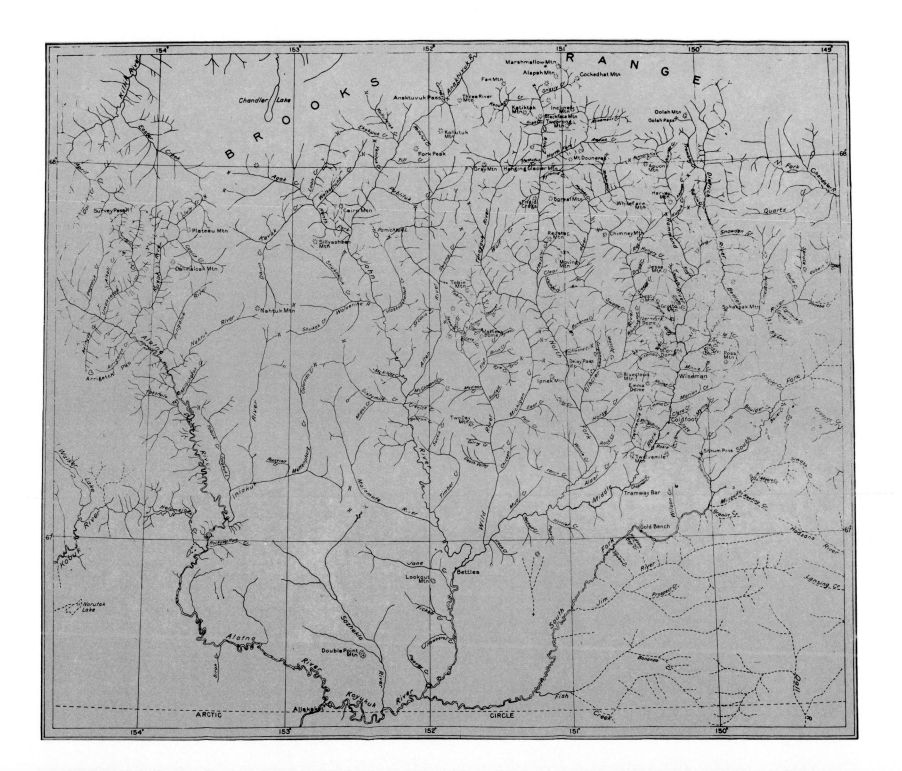

(Above ↕) *Jim Kelly (right) holds a pulley during efforts to raise Sam Dubin's Cat which had broken through the ice on the Koyukuk at Wiseman. This Cat, photographed here in the early 1930s, was the first one in Koyukuk country.* (Courtesy of William English, Jr.)

(Right →) *Prospectors Bill Gilbert (left) and Knute Ellingson were longtime partners in the mines around Wiseman.* (Courtesy of Tishu Ulen)

Miners operate a hydraulic giant at Sam O'Brien's placer operation along Porcupine Creek, which enters the Middle Fork Koyukuk River south of Coldfoot. (Courtesy of William English, Jr.)

Using a Caterpillar tractor, a miner rechannels water that has come through a sluice box at this placer operation. The hydraulic giant in the background washes overburden to the top of the sluice. Then, as the water carries the gravel down the sluice, gold, which is heavier than the gravel, collects at the bottom of the sluice and is later gathered up by the miners. (Courtesy of William English, Jr.)

Residents of Wiseman await the arrival of the first river scow of the season about 1912 or 1913.
(Courtesy of Tishu Ulen)

The Old Ways

Many of the old-time Eskimo customs were dying out about the time I was born. Long ago when an older person died they would make a platform and set the body, wrapped in clothing, on it. A full year later materials would be gathered for garments. The women would tan and sew for a whole month making clothing for those who had helped during the last illness and burial. Then they would gather food for a feast, but first would come the singing and garment giving. The men and women who were to receive gifts would be lined up on one side of the igloo. A new garment would be held up, and then, with singing, it would be placed in front of the person honored. After the feast came more singing and dancing. Sometimes other villages contributed. After the white people came, this celebration died out and was replaced by funerals.

There weren't any wedding ceremonies. The big thing was getting the girl. A young girl stayed with her mother until someone wanted her for a daughter-in-law. The boy's parents would generally ask for the girl. The boy and girl had nothing to say about it. The girl would be around 14 or 15, and the boy around 17. A few boys remained bachelors, but not many.

Most arranged marriages worked out pretty well. The boy would come to live with the girl's family for a while, but after the first baby arrived, they'd build their own igloo and become a separate family. In the old days a good hunter had two wives, or even three. If he traveled a lot he would take the young wife with him. The wives got along very well. They lived in the same igloo and helped one another with their children.

Pregnant women were physically active right up until their babies were born, and then they were in labor only an hour or so. Those who didn't want a big baby would often wear a belt to keep it from growing too much.

According to custom, women were supposed to have their babies alone. When my mother had her first baby, she had to go out into the woods about three-quarters of a mile from the village. My grandmother dug out a place in the snow and put down dry hay. Then she built a big bonfire. My grandfather kept it going. They didn't worry much about custom, I guess, because my grandmother stayed right beside her. When the baby was born, they cut the cord with an *ulu* and tied it with sinew. Then they wiped the baby off with pieces of skin. In four days my mother returned to the village with her baby.

Sometimes a mother would die and another mother would nurse the baby. If no nursing mothers were around, the baby would be fed fish or meat broth. A baby would sometimes get pot-bellied from the broth but would usually come through. It must have been hard to feed babies because food had to be chewed first and then transferred from mouth to mouth.

For diapers they used a little piece of skin with moss inside. The moss from dry lakes had little feathers in it and had no smell like cloth diapers. At least there wasn't much washing. When traveling they carried along lots of moss that had been gathered in the summer.

There was very little fighting among my people because they were busy gathering food and didn't have time to quarrel. There wasn't any stealing that I knew of, probably because none of us had much to steal. If they were hungry, people just helped themselves to whatever they could find. Everyone shared what they had. If a woman lost her husband, the men of the group would provide her with meat and skins. And if she couldn't raise her family alone, different families would adopt the children.

Mama was six or seven when her father died suddenly at a fishing camp in Kobuk country. Mama never knew just how old she was or what year her father died, but the following year her

Judge Cecil Clegg holds naturalization ceremonies for new citizens of the United States at Wiseman in July 1928. Tishu Ulen, holding her baby, stands in the front row. (Courtesy of Tishu Ulen)

mother died, leaving four young children. Many other Eskimos died that same year from an unknown disease. An elderly couple in the area gathered up 16 orphans and cared for them through the winter. In the spring word reached the relatives, and they arrived to pick up the children for adoption.

Adoption was very common, but there were some strict rules to be followed. It was important for children to know where they came from, and adopted children were always carefully taught about their own families. Blood ties were never forgotten. If the adoptive parents died, the children were always told to go back to their own people. Everyone kept close track of families for several generations back.

It was against the rules for close blood relations to marry. Even marriage between adopted children was frowned upon. It was understood that inter-marriage between blood relations was not good for the people. A few cousins did marry, but this was rare. I don't remember seeing retarded or defective babies. We traded with the Indians, but were not allowed to marry them.

Some families had 10 or more children. The children were given chores quite early in life. The girls gathered wood, packed water, and learned to cook and sew. The boys went hunting with their fathers, and learned to make snowshoes and sleds. Everyone had something to do. If a boy's father died, an Eskimo friend or relative would teach him all about hunting. My boy was trained to stalk game by Sammy Hope.

There was little or no spanking among Eskimo mothers. Instead they would talk to their children. I remember how we'd get in a circle, then sit down and listen. The older people would tell us the way life was supposed to go for 30 minutes to an hour, and then would tell us to go play and think about it. I was taught to listen whenever my mother spoke to me.

The children played games together and didn't usually quarrel very much. As they grew up they learned to get along well with people, and most of our people were happy people. If a young woman made trouble, the old women would get together and talk to her. But they'd always go as a group rather than one alone, and it generally worked.

Our igloos were not ice houses as shown in children's geography books. The igloos were made from cottonwood, which is easy to split. We would dig about three feet down, and then build up the walls. The roof was slanted with an opening on top to let the smoke out. The door was kept cracked to make a draft. You could stand up straight in most igloos. They were light inside because of the white of the cottonwood. There were big bunches of moss and dirt for insulation, and after the evening meal the coals would be covered up to hold the warmth. It would be so warm you could take off your parky.

Of course, different people made igloos in different ways. On the arctic coast they used driftwood for the frame. Inland Eskimos used caribou skin tents for traveling. Dried wood was tied together for a frame. When on the trail, people tried to make camp where there were green willows as well as fresh water. Hot rocks, laid on green willows, would keep the tent warm at night. A chunk of ice from a lake or river was tied with rawhide and hung up inside the igloo to melt, supplying drinking water.

Suppertime was the main meal, and everyone would sit in a circle. The mother would dish up the food out of big wooden platters that had been carved out of spruce wood with flint knives. Before iron pots were available, food was cooked in wooden buckets hollowed out of a log. Rocks were heated in the fire, then placed in water in the wooden bucket. The water would get hot from the rocks. When the second hot rocks were put in, the food simmered until ready to eat. Cooking was done inside the igloo in winter to help keep it warm all evening.

Most of the old-time Eskimos knew what it was to be hungry. My mother knew. She told me about one winter while trekking, when they had been a long time without food. They were getting weak. My grandmother told her son, my daddy, to take Mama and her sister down to the timber to see if they could find food for the girls. When asked about herself and her husband, she said, "We've lived long enough. Find food for the girls." Grandpa never said a word. I guess he would have stayed there and starved to death. He always did what Grandma told him to do. Anyhow, during the night the boys went out once more and this time they got 11 caribou. My daddy brought a big pack of meat into the tent. Grandma started cooking the meat right away. She fed the girls first because she had just two, her own daughter and my mother who was adopted, but she had five sons. In later years my mother put more value on boys than girls.

Small groups of maybe two families traveled together. Often the groups would meet because they followed the same general routes. They were always glad to see one another and share whatever they had. There was little selfishness among the old-time Eskimos.

A tram carries Bill English, Jr. (right), and Price Hopson across the Koyukuk River about a mile below Wiseman. (Courtesy of William English, Jr.)

59

Food and Healing

Hunting was the most important part of our lives because from hunting came not only our food but clothing and dog food and tools from bone. Every part of an animal had use. Our people, the Kobuk Eskimos, had followed the caribou herds as long as anyone could remember. The caribou would almost always be at the Canadian border in May right after the snow was gone. As a girl my mother had trekked clear across Alaska several times. When I was a girl, the caribou still came through the Arctic. You could see them like a moving cloud. The Eskimo custom was to let the first caribou go by so the herd would not turn away. Then they would keep on coming. A cow and calf would generally lead the herd.

We all liked caribou meat the best, but we ate a lot of moose too. Caribou seemed to be the most nourishing for people and dogs. There were plenty of sheep around, but one meal of sheep was usually plenty. Sheep is the poorest meat to try to live on. You get filled up fast, but in 30 minutes you are hungry again because sheep have no fat on them.

A change of meat helped break the monotony. We used a spring pole to hang rabbits in a snare. We also snared birds, mostly ptarmigan. No bait was used. We never ate wolverine or wolf meat though some arctic people did. And we didn't have much to do with bear. According to custom, only people older than 50 were allowed to eat bear meat. Once, a brown bear bit my Uncle Isaac and his skin began to turn white. In later years my son asked me, "How come you never told me I had a white uncle at Noorvik?" Another Eskimo in Barrow ate

Holding his family's supper, Joe Ulen is surrounded by his three children, (from left) Florence, Ben, and Mary. A neighbor, young George Tobuk, stands in front of Mary in this 1935 photo taken at Wiseman. (Courtesy of Tishu Ulen)

polar bear liver and turned white also . . . as white as can be. I can't explain it.

Our people were careful not to waste anything. Wolf and wolverine skins were always highly prized. Even the caribou hooves were used to carve spoons, and horns were used for fishnet sinkers. Sinew from the caribou back was used for thread.

We used to eat meat raw after it was seasoned for a while. If the hunters got the meat early in the fall, they put out poles and laid the meat on it. Then they put rocks on it to keep other animals from getting it. The air circulated through the meat to keep it from spoiling. You had to learn to eat it, however. The dogs usually had their meat raw and were kept well fed when working. Sometimes a broth was made for them when we were short of meat.

Before our people had guns, and later, when they ran out of shells, they used spears or bows and arrows. A good hunter had to be able to run fast. Eskimos also carried their own flint for building fires. They'd take grass (Alaska cotton) or dried hay wrapped in a loon skin, which was absolutely waterproof. It was important to take good care of the flint, which was a hard rock that came from up in the Arctic. It could make the difference between life and death. But the coming of matches made life a lot easier for our people.

Good sleds and snowshoes were another part of successful hunting. These were usually made in the summertime, the sleds of lightweight birch which didn't even have to be seasoned. Usually men made the tools and women made the clothing, but not necessarily. My aunt Annie made excellent snowshoes as well as *ulus* with bone or sheep horn. The *ulu* blades were made from a saw, tied to the handle with rawhide, and dried over heat.

Inland Eskimos ate different foods from coastal Eskimos. My mother tasted her first seal oil on a trip to Barrow when she was quite young. She wasn't used to oily foods such as whale meat and seal, and she soon found they were too rich for her

To break the monotony of a constant diet of red meat, Tishu snared ptarmigan, such as this willow ptarmigan, shown here in fall plumage.
(Brad Ebel)

and she couldn't eat. Her family began to worry that she would starve to death, so they headed up the Colville River to look for caribou. Arctic fish — grayling, lingcod, whitefish — were tasty and abundant and could tide them over until they reached caribou country.

Usually in early spring we had lean days, but once the fish started running in the rivers, we ate well again. But to catch the fish, we had to make nets from willow bark. It took all spring to make the nets. Everyone worked on the nets, and everyone used them. When the sap was running, the willow bark was stripped from the trees. Then the bark was split and twisted into nets 30 to 40 feet long. They were fastened to the bank on one end; the other end was fastened to a boat or raft that moved slowly downstream. We'd get salmon, grayling, pinhead, lush, and big whitefish. This was the old-time Eskimo way of seining.

To Mama money didn't mean much, but food was everything. I remember a story she told in the early days of the gold rush to the Koyukuk. My father and mother were camped between Middle Fork and Hammond River. My daddy got two moose way up in the creek, butchered them, and then came upon a mining hole sunk in the middle of a dry creek where some white men were working. Daddy couldn't speak English, but he held up two fingers and pointed up the creek from where he'd come. The next day he returned to haul the meat out and found a lot of white men with a tripod and scales to weigh the meat. And there was a gold scale, too. My father tried to tell the miners he had a wife and child waiting, but nobody paid any attention. They were hungry. Finally, he grabbed up a chunk of meat they were cutting up and held onto it. When they got through with the moose, all he had left were two heads, eight legs, and the piece of meat in his hands. He drove his four dogs back to camp where Mama met him with, "What happened to the meat?" My father showed her the poke of gold dust the miners gave him. She was disgusted and said, "You eat it." They decided they'd better get away from there fast. They left at daybreak the next day, went up the river, and fortunately got another moose. This time they hung the hindquarters and liver, ate all they could, and stayed as far away as possible from miners.

The white people who came into the country had a problem with scurvy. Their gums would turn black. We Eskimos didn't have this problem because we lived off fresh meat. We also used

Early people of the Koyukuk stuffed Alaska cotton (shown here) into a loon skin to make a safe, waterproof carrying pouch for their flint which was needed for making fires. Before matches were brought into Koyukuk country, a good flint could mean the difference between life and death.
(Michael S. Wright)

Above ↑) Bill English, Jr. (left), and Dave Titus carry out a caribou to replenish their meat supply. Throughout the decades, caribou have migrated through Koyukuk country from wintering grounds south of the Brooks Range to calving grounds on the arctic slope. (Courtesy of William English, Jr.)

(Above ↑) *Mrs. Mary English and Bill, Jr., pick cranberries on Lookout Mountain (2,118 feet) about three and a half miles southwest of Bettles.* (Courtesy of William English, Jr.)

(Right →) *Ben Ulen enjoys a hunting outing at Big Lake, between Bettles River and the South Fork Koyukuk River, in fall 1953.* (Courtesy of Tishu Ulen)

Labrador tea, wild rhubarb, willow shoots, and Alaska potatoes, which were roots we gathered in the fall and kept through the winter. Spruce gum was knocked off the trees in clusters and was in much demand as a tonic for the kidneys. Spruce gum was traded along with furs at Barrow in exchange for cartridges and tea that came right off the boats.

There were many kinds of treatments for illness among the Eskimo people. My mama had learned about medicine men and their treatments through her uncle. The teaching came down from generation to generation in some families.

Seal oil was a cure-all. Sometimes it was used for earaches. Other times it would be given to drink like castor oil. To dry up cuts or sores on the skin, puffballs were gathered and dried in the fall to be used during the winter. Puffballs were also delicious when fried and eaten, but we never ate other mushrooms. And then rose hips were gathered when ripe and eaten raw. No one knew anything about vitamin C, but everyone knew that rose hips satisfied a certain craving and were good. And for a purgative or a tonic, Labrador tea was dried and then boiled and taken as a rather bitter tea. Nature provided medicine for everything. Spruce gum cleaned the teeth when chewed, was used on cuts to aid healing, and was supposed to help little boys stay dry at night. When you'd cut your hand, you'd take a piece of skin from a new caribou hide and wrap it around the cut as a bandage. It was just like a modern Band-Aid.

We had no dentists and no cavities in the early days. Everyone I knew had good, even teeth. There weren't any toothbrushes, but we chewed spruce gum and dried meat and gave the teeth lots of exercise. Many people died with all their teeth still in their head, though some of the old women wore their teeth down to the gums from shaping *oogruk* bottoms for mukluks. Today they save the teeth by using pliers to make boots.

I don't remember anyone having chicken pox, measles, or mumps. I was almost 50 when I finally got measles in Fairbanks. I thought I would die, I was so sick. What sickness we had in those early days usually came in the spring when the boats and barges came with freight from Outside, and more people began traveling up and down the rivers. Then came colds, flu, and pneumonia.

In April 1923 a flu epidemic hit the Koyukuk. Some people used quinine, but we had nothing. I woke up in the night with bleeding from my nose and ears. Mama thought my baby brother would die, so to keep him evenly warm, she kept him under her parky for a whole week. When I began to get well, Mama sent me out to gather sand and feathers from a swallow's nest near the roof of our cabin in Wiseman. She took the sand and feathers into the bedroom. Whatever she did with them, my baby brother grew lively and began eating again. After the flu I discovered that I could see the birds moving their mouths, but I couldn't hear the songs anymore. Much of my hearing was gone.

I remember the time Mama treated Harry Snowden, an Eskimo friend, for boils on the back. She took fine charcoal from the stove and chewed it in her mouth. She told him, "Now hold still" and blew the charcoal right down his back. Then she put a bandage over it and prayed. The next day the boils broke, drained, and disappeared.

The time I was laid up with a swollen knee from a bad fall, Mama came back from Fairbanks, looked at me, and took a small knife in her hand. She poked the knife into my knee in two places. My knee drained and healed up quickly.

Mama delivered many babies, and she preferred the Eskimo style of delivery. Instead of letting the mother lie down, she'd have her squat quietly in a sitting position and bear down. Then she would catch the baby as it arrived. She would cut the cord and tie it with sinew. She kept the mother in the same position until her stomach became hard, and the mother would be up and about quickly.

When I was born, my eyes filmed over. Mama

Eskimos of the upper Koyukuk used Labrador tea (left) and rose hips (below) to ward off scurvy, a disease caused by a deficiency of vitamin C. The rose hips were collected when ripe and eaten raw; the tea was dried, then boiled to make a bitter brew.
(Both by John and Margaret Ibbotson)

was afraid I would go blind if the film hardened, so she took two long hairs from her head, boiled them, and rubbed my eyes with the hairs. She rubbed the left eye harder than the right eye. I have had trouble with it all through my life. The eye doctor told me that my eye was injured when I was small. He never asked me what happened, but I knew. It wasn't a very common operation among the Eskimos, but it usually worked in a way similar to a cataract operation today. Most people had good eyesight, but one old lady who was blind from birth was able to make beautiful boots by using her fingertips.

The old-time Eskimos didn't understand why people would dry up and die with cancer or cough to death with tuberculosis. These were white men's diseases. If men survived hunting accidents, they usually died of old age. A few may have had something like appendicitis though we didn't know what it was. We always tried to take care of our own people.

There was a man in Kobuk country who lived on and on, even after his grandchildren were old. The young folks of the village would take turns coming in and chewing his food for him. Young people were taught to respect and take care of the old and helpless. When the man finally died, everyone said he was older than anyone who had ever lived.

Medicine Men and Missionaries

Before the coming of the white man, the people believed in *dooneraks,* good and bad spirits. The medicine man knew how to handle *dooneraks,* and he was as strong as the spirits he commanded. A strong medicine man was supposed to be able to heal people, control weather, visit with the dead, and perhaps look into the future. If he died, his powers would go to someone else in his family.

My mama's uncle Peluk was considered a great medicine man. He had never heard of Christianity. He told Mama if she ever got sick to come to him right away. He lived about a day's walk from her. She got a pain in her heel which seemed to get worse and worse. Finally she got a friend to help her walk to the home of her uncle. She got there late in the day and told her uncle that her heel was painful. He didn't say anything, but after supper he took out his drum and laid it under her heel. Then he took a hollow stick and began to suck on it. Slowly, she saw a woman's long hair come out of her heel. Then he pulled it out all the way. He never said how it got there. In about a week she went home running and never had trouble with her heel again.

After my mother was orphaned, she became helpless with a bad back. My father's mother wanted a daughter, even though my mother was an invalid. Mama was carried to my grandmother's igloo on a new caribou hide, and there she was tended for two years. One of her treatments was to be propped up and to listen to drumming. The sound of the drums was supposed to take away evil spirits. Whatever helped, her back healed perfectly, and she was able to lead an active and useful life.

Another story she told me happened a long time ago in the Kobuk. Mama and Nakuchluk, Peluk's wife, were driving their dogs along the river on the way home from a meat-hauling trip. They were on glare ice and making good time. Suddenly a ball of fire went by them and then turned back. Mama was scared. Nakuchluk said, "Don't be afraid. That's only your uncle who came to see how we were getting along." When they got home to the village, the other women told them their uncle Peluk had said he had seen them coming on the river and that they would be in that night.

I think my mother first learned of Christianity in Kobuk country. Someone had picked up the white man's words and translated them into Eskimo. The old-time people had been dependent on the medicine men. After missionaries came, the people began dropping the old beliefs, although I think some people practiced both. Big Jim was a good Christian and also a good medicine man. One time Mama had a bad headache. Big Jim treated her by blowing in her ear. She said she felt that he blew right through her head, and then the headache was gone. Big Jim always used his power for healing and helping others.

Some of our people became Christians, but not all. Those who really believed in Christ seemed happy and would pray for the sick. Mama prayed over a lot of things. When I didn't feel well, she would make tea, then pray over it and give it to me to drink.

I think the Eskimo people believed in life after death even before they ever heard about Christianity. I remember an old story from my mother's days about a man who died, stayed dead four days, and then came back to life to tell about it. He told beautiful stories about where he'd been after death. I can't tell all he said, but he lived a long time before he died the next time. I guess he came back so he could report. But the place he went was beautiful.

The Jonas cabin stands on the outskirts of Wiseman near the airport. A stove is set up outside for summer cooking. This cabin was built by Big Jim and occupied by him and his wife, Nakuchluk, in the 1920s and 1930s. The cabin later passed to the Jonas family. (Walter Johnson)

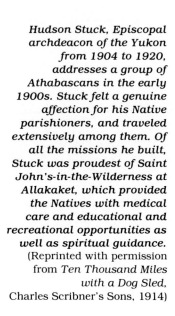

The old Eskimo people were a happy people and never afraid to die. But they felt it was their responsibility to teach young people how to live.

Another story is one I saw for myself. Mama, Mrs. Jonas, and I were walking on a trail near Wiseman late one night when suddenly Mama stopped and said, "Did you hear something?" We said, "No." She said, "It came from this side," and she pointed toward Big Lake, which was about 30 miles to the east. "It sounded like a woman crying," Mama said. She heard it twice. We looked at the clock when we reached her house to make tea. Two days later Nakuchluk arrived in Wiseman by sled with her husband's body. He had died of a heart attack the night that Mama heard the crying. Nakuchluk told my mother, "I cried so hard that night." "I heard you!" my mother answered.

Perhaps she inherited some of her uncle Peluk's talents.

Some of our people adopted the Christian faith wholeheartedly. I remember the story of a Christian Eskimo couple whose adopted son died while they were trekking in the Arctic. They made a little sled and hauled his body way over to Christian River north of Fort Yukon, and then back to Hammond River. They found a place where the sun wouldn't hit, dug a tunnel into the mountain, and lined it with moss. They built a small platform, placed the son's body on it, and closed the tunnel with trees and boulders so that animals couldn't get in during the summer. After freezeup in the fall, they hauled the body to Bettles for a proper Christian service and burial by the missionaries. That's how strongly they believed.

Saint John's-in-the-Wilderness, the Episcopal mission at Allakaket, was built in 1907 by Archdeacon Hudson Stuck. The church served the Indians of Allakaket as well as the Eskimos of Alatna, across the river. (Reprinted with permission from *Voyages on the Yukon and Its Tributaries*, Charles Scribner's Sons, 1917)

I was baptized by Archdeacon Hudson Stuck at Saint John's-in-the-Wilderness in 1910. My parents traveled there especially for my baptism. Saint John's-in-the-Wilderness was a comfortable log building that served as a church, nursing facilities, and living quarters for women missionaries who taught and nursed the people of the Koyukuk. Miss Carter was the first one, and later came Miss Ridgeway, Miss Pomfrey, Miss Hill, and Miss Kay. They held Sunday school classes, and a priest traveling by dog team held church services regularly. Whenever we were near, we would go to church on Sunday. We all looked forward to services when Archdeacon Stuck came in. Reverend Crane and Bishop Bentley covered our part of the country after Hudson Stuck left.

Most Eskimos believed in God and Jesus Christ, but I don't think they understood much beyond the Ten Commandments. That really got to them. They talked among themselves about hell and heaven and the Crucifixion, and often spoke of Jesus' coming like a returning hunter. They really enjoyed the singing in church, and the celebrations brought happiness and variety to their lives.

When Mrs. Louisa Pingel, an ex-missionary, moved with her miner husband to Nolan Creek, she began holding regular Sunday meetings in the Pioneer Hall in Wiseman. She would walk the seven miles from Nolan to Wiseman in every kind of weather to teach Bible stories to the people. Everyone was welcome. The people liked her and attended her services quite regularly, especially when Big Jim was in town. Big Jim had a strong influence on the Eskimo people at Wiseman.

Angel of Allakaket

By Shirley English

A strange twist of circumstances brought Miss Amelia Hill to Alaska instead of China. Fate, or perhaps Providence, kept her there until the spell of Koyukuk country held her fast for 30 years.

The hazel-eyed Irish lass from Tralee had just completed her nurses' training in Pittsburgh when she was pressed into service to tend the sick and dying during the 1918 flu epidemic. That experience gave her a taste for public service that led her to the mission field in the Episcopal church.

Two years of additional training for mission work followed. The young nurse studied Chinese. Her trunks were packed and tickets ready when an impulsive act changed the course of her life. The simple act of applying for United States citizenship made her legally ineligible to go to China for four years. Deeply disappointed, she returned to school, this time in Philadelphia.

Bishop Peter Trimble Rowe of Alaska was in Philadelphia. He suggested that Miss Hill wait out the next four years at Saint John's-in-the-Wilderness at Allakaket. The remote mission on the Arctic Circle, founded by Archdeacon Hudson Stuck in 1907, served not only the hundred villagers clustered near the church, but also served as a religious center for 600 miles along the Koyukuk River.

Miss Hill traveled first to the log cabin city of Fairbanks, where pioneer Mrs. Eva McGown from Ireland took her under her wing. Bishop Rowe, Arthur Wright, Johnnie Fredson, and Miss Hill were aboard the mission boat *Pelican II* as it floated down the Tanana and Yukon rivers, then slowly chugged up the Koyukuk until the passengers reached the cross-tipped mission of rough-hewn logs at Allakaket. Beside the mission clustered moss-chinked Indian cabins which faced the Eskimo village of Alatna across the Koyukuk at the confluence of the Alatna River.

The rivers were vital to village economy in Alaska in 1922. They were highways through the wilderness for summer and winter travel. In summer, the rivers yielded a harvest of salmon; in winter, trappers took beaver from beneath the river ice. At breakup, the rivers were a threat to the villagers. The mission at Saint John's had to be rebuilt when the swift current of the Koyukuk undercut the bank.

Miss Hill soon found nursing only a part of her duties. She tagged beavers, acted as postmaster, delivered babies, tended to those on welfare, and served as the dentist in emergencies. Extracting teeth without anesthetic was a painful chore. "I suffered more than the people. My knees always shook when it was over," she confessed.

She also conducted church services from behind the birch lectern, an Indian interpreter on one side, an Eskimo on the other. "The friendly competition between the two peoples kept life interesting," observed Miss Hill. "They are a gracious people with an old culture, considerate of one another's feelings, and nature's true gentlemen. I found them remarkably artistic with an ability to see, not just look. I learned much from them."

Every spring Miss Hill superintended ice-cutting, marshaling drivers and dogs to fill the ice house for the summer. And when local springs trickled dry in autumn, Miss Hill piloted the mission motorboat up the nearby Alatna River to bring back fresh, cold water. When smallpox broke out on the lower Yukon, she worked night and day in the stricken villages with sharp needles and soft voice to protect hundreds by vaccination. Her deeds of mercy won the confidence of Natives and sourdoughs alike. "Miss Hill" became a title of respect and love as well as a name to countless Alaskans.

In the mid-1950s, Miss Amelia Hill visits with her friends Tishu (center) and Joe Ulen in Fairbanks.
(Courtesy of Shirley English)

Life along the Koyukuk had its dramatic moments. One Sunday afternoon about 1926 the villagers were playing kickball in the snow. Suddenly, out of the overcast sky lumbered an airplane that circled the village. Old Sitsoo hid under her skins, and dogs disappeared in the woods. Awe-stricken, the villagers watched their first airplane. Two notes dropped by the pilot fell into the river. The third message was retrieved. It read, "What river is this?" What village? Which way to Fairbanks?" Hastily, with precious black fuel, the people of Allakaket wrote on the snow, "Fairbanks, southeast," but the plane kept circling. The pilot didn't understand. Finally little Frank Tobuk's suggestion saved the day. He had everyone get in line like a human arrow and point to the southeast. They did. Wings rocking in thanks, the plane headed straight for Fairbanks. Later in the spring, the people of Allakaket learned that Capt. George H. (later Sir Hubert) Wilkins and Carl Ben Eielson had reached Fairbanks safely from their polar flight.

Miss Hill's appreciation for the fun-filled Eskimos and the quiet, dignified Indians who worshiped together at Saint John's grew as the years passed swiftly. Miss Bessie Kay, a mission schoolteacher, arrived in 1932 to become Miss Hill's co-worker for 20 years. The lady missionaries encouraged fishing and trapping. The children learned English and became bilingual but were urged not to lose their own language. The mission was a center for worship and education, and also for cultural activities such as dances and stories handed down for hundreds, perhaps thousands of years. Leaders such as Chief Moses, Big William, Johnny Oldman, and Frank Tobuk offered their support.

At the end of four years, Miss Hill had discovered that her first four years of residency were invalid. She went back to the Koyukuk for another four years. By the time she had fulfilled the requirements of citizenship, Miss Hill's hair had silvered and her life had become rooted in the Arctic. In Judge Cecil Clegg's special court session in Fairbanks in 1936, Miss Hill at last became a United States citizen. Noel Wien, Dixie Hall, and Otto Geist were her witnesses. "Twas a proud day," she recalled. Another proud occasion was the day she received life membership in the Pioneers of Alaska.

Eluknigasooli, meaning "sometime again" was the fond farewell in 1953 when Miss Hill retired and left Alaska. The people whom she had loved and served so long and faithfully knew that she would always be a part of their lives as they reaped the harvest of her efforts throughout the years. Miss Amelia Hill had left her mark on living history in Koyukuk country.

Eskimo Entertainment

The Eskimo village was always fun for children because there were games going on all the time. A football type of game was played in my mother's time. A ball was made of caribou hide and stuffed with caribou hair, which made it bouncy. A field would be laid out with a goal set up on each end. I don't remember the rules, but this game was played in wintertime and often late at night. This was an Eskimo game for adults, not children, but I can still see them out there having a good time. Another game was for summertime with a smaller ball stuffed with hair. This game was a kind of handball played with two evenly divided teams.

The high kick was popular. A mitt would be hung from a line, and people would take turns kicking it. Gradually the mitt would be raised. Both feet had to touch the mitt to score. I remember an old lady who could kick higher than almost anyone.

Some of us would fall over backward trying to reach that mitt, and in the process nearly tear down the tent. Those who had learned the high kick long ago, like my mother, seemed to do better than the younger ones.

Another game we used to play in the igloo in the wintertime was a throwing game. Someone would place a stake in the center of the igloo. We were given two sticks per person. Whoever threw closest to the stake got so many numbers. The Eskimo name for that game was *kipitoruk*. There were a lot of other games, but in Wiseman the Eskimo games gradually became mixed with white men's games like pitching horseshoes.

When different villages came together, they used to hold masquerades. There were prizes given for the best. Sometimes they'd use wooden masks. Mama told me about one winter long ago when her people were having a masquerade and dance at their Alatna River camp. The people were taking a

Nellie McNeal enjoys a perennial pastime of the young-at-heart at Bettles.
(Courtesy of Tishu Ulen)

72

break at midnight when they heard a strange tinkling and rattling noise. It came closer and closer up to the igloo, and everyone sat silently listening. Whatever it was came to the door . . . and there was a man on hands and knees with icicles hanging from his beard. His frozen clothing rattled when he moved. His feet and hands were frozen. He was helped into the igloo where the Eskimos gave him broth and cut off his sealskin boots. All that night he moaned and groaned, but the next morning he was wrapped in furs, loaded on a sled, and driven by two Eskimo boys to Bergman, about 100 miles away. From Bergman they took him to the hospital at Fort Gibbon at the mouth of the Tanana River. This happened about the time the white people first came into the country. No one ever learned the man's name because no one spoke any English. We only knew he had been traveling alone from across the Kobuk River. He came back the next year in pretty good shape. Mama said if he had been in their Eskimo masquerade, he would have won first prize that night.

Guessing games were also popular indoor games. We'd pick something out of the woods, and everyone had to guess what it was. Whoever guessed right got a prize.

I always remember those winter evenings when we played outdoors on bright moonlit nights. We used caribou hides to slide over the ice. One place we played, we'd slide as fast as possible behind one another, and shove that person in the water if he didn't get away fast. We'd sit on the fur and slide on the skin side. Most of our games were tests of skill or quickness.

When the ice on the Koyukuk River was smooth, we'd get on a big sled and put up a piece of canvas for a sail. Off we'd go down the river for about three miles, all bundled up and having a wonderful time. The hard part came when we had to drag the sled back upstream on the slippery ice with all the little

Bill English, Jr. (right), and Henry Hope play with pups at Bettles. (Courtesy of William English, Jr.)

73

Four youngsters from Wiseman, (from left) Frank Minano, Bill English, Jr., Joseph Hope, and Oscar Jonas, are dressed for playing in the winter snow outside the schoolhouse in 1932. (Courtesy of William English, Jr.)

children on it. We could only make about two trips because it took so long to get back along the edge of the ice.

When we went to school in Coldfoot, we had one pair of ice skates that strapped on our boots. All 11 of us took turns learning to skate, and some of us got pretty good. We skated on the smooth river overflow ice. Eskimo children learn early in life to get along together and share.

Songs, dances, games, and stories helped fill the long winter evenings. Eskimo songs were usually about hunting or fishing. They were all from memory because nothing was ever written down. Some people made up their own songs. Some songs were funny, some told stories, and some were just chanting. The songs have changed over the years — I guess the difference in subjects reflects the changing life of our people.

Whenever we would hear a drum beating, we'd hurry over to dance. The old folks used to dance almost every night, summer and winter. The men

and women always wore gloves when dancing. It's been that way since it all began. When a dancer hands you a glove, you have to get out and dance. Another custom is for Eskimo men to wear a loon-skin when dancing. They take the loon's bill and tie it around the back of their head with two feathers. I don't know what it means other than being an old custom. Eskimos dance in one place rather than moving around, probably because the igloo wasn't large enough to allow for several people to move at the same time.

The songs and dances meant a lot to my people. When my mama was dying, she sang Big Jim's song about Wiseman. In English it went like this:

I am lonesome,
I want to feel better.
I want to warm myself,
So I go to Wiseman.
I go.
All of us go.
All of us sing. . . .

School Days

Although Mama taught me sewing and other things, she wanted me to go to a regular school. In 1919 I started to school in Coldfoot. The teacher, Miss Vanda Ruth Coffey, had 12 students from ages 6 to 19. Miss Coffey was a single lady from Oregon, but she lasted just two years before she married Jesse Allen, a miner and camp cook.

The next teacher was Mrs. Mary Glenn. She had taught at Bettles, where there had been a big school. Then she married a scow man, Bill Glenn, and moved Outside. But Bill loved the Koyukuk country and came back to work his mining ground around 1915. Mary took over the Coldfoot school in 1921 and taught for two years. She was quite old and white-haired, but she had lots of energy and loved her students. She taught us with books all day, and in the evenings and on weekends we learned about cooking and homemaking. She never tired of teaching.

Those were happy days. She believed young people had a need to learn practical things. Three of us girls would go to her place on Saturday mornings to wash dishes and clothes. We learned to starch blouses, iron, and clean the house. On Sunday we'd have a taffy pull and dance. Mary Glenn taught us to dance to an old Edison crank-up phonograph with a roll. We learned waltzes and two-steps and even square dances. Mrs. Glenn wanted her girls to be ladies. She even taught us to cross our legs gracefully when seated. She supervised everything we did, but was right there

One of the teachers in the early days of formal education in the upper Koyukuk was Mrs. Mary Glenn. She taught at the big school at Bettles until she married Bill Glenn, who ran a scow on the river. The Glenns moved Outside but later returned to the Koyukuk. Mrs. Glenn was the teacher at Coldfoot from 1921 to 1923. (Courtesy of Tishu Ulen)

Teacher Clara Carpenter (back row, center) poses in front of the Wiseman school with her students in about 1930. (Courtesy of William English, Jr.)

Mr. Turner stands with his students at the Wiseman School about 1938.
(Courtesy of Tishu Ulen)

laughing and enjoying every step. From her I learned everything about homemaking.

Eventually the Glenns moved back Outside, and Helen Crane became teacher for one year. After that the school was closed because Coldfoot was dying. About 1925 the school building was towed on a sled to thriving Wiseman. It is still there today, a nice log building with a big stove. There's a view over the mountains through two big windows in the back. When it arrived, it was the best building in Wiseman. My children went to the same school I did, and it was full of happy memories. The school stayed open until the 1940s, when everybody took off for Fairbanks, and the village seemed deserted.

Miss McElroy was the first teacher in Wiseman. Then Miss Lavery came in. To hold a school, a community had to have two half-white children and at least eight students in those days, so my little Florence had to go to school when she was only four. When she got sleepy, the teacher would hold her for her nap.

The teacher's quarters were in a separate building in front of the school, and they were kept comfortable and warm. A janitor kept the fires going in the schoolhouse and hauled drinking water for the children. The water was kept in a big can with a dipper.

The school became a center for the town. Everyone enjoyed the programs and holidays there. I remember one Christmas program where my four-year-old Florence was all dressed up and recited *The Night Before Christmas*. The pilot S.E. Robbins thought she was so cute that he grabbed her up and kissed her. She didn't like that at all and screamed to go home. But going to school so young didn't hurt Florence because she learned so much from the older children.

Sometimes there were as many as 12 students, but they would come and go with the hunting and trapping seasons. It was a big job for one teacher, especially when there were students who couldn't speak English. Even my mother went to school one winter.

Clara Carpenter was there for a while, followed by George Rayburn for two or three years. Mrs. Long was the last teacher, and then the school was closed. Some of the children besides mine were Kitty, Lucy, Oscar, and Harry Jonas; Nellie Riley, Billy English, Jr., Price Harding, and Charlie Horner.

Life In Wiseman

The gold camp of Wiseman was an exciting place to live when I was young. Everyone turned out for the dances, and miners and trappers came from miles around. The dancing season started with Thanksgiving, followed by Christmas and New Year's, then Washington's Birthday and Saint Patrick's Day, which was the last dance until the Fourth of July. On the Fourth we'd have a shoot, with a prize for the best shot, and a pie-eating contest. Speeches were delivered by old-timers from the creeks, and even the Eskimos would get into the act and make a speech in their own language with someone translating for them. Around election time in the fall, the miners would head for town for another big day.

When I was a schoolgirl in Coldfoot, we used to drive the 11 miles by dog sled in the moonlight to dance in Wiseman. I sometimes danced from 8:00 P.M. until time to hitch up the dogs and head back to Coldfoot at 8:00 A.M. There were waltzes, two-steps, schottisches, and square dances. The Eskimos would do their own dances two or three times in the evening. The white people would get up and try the Eskimo dancing for fun. We danced to an old wind-up Victrola or an old piano in the Pioneers' Hall, Igloo #8. Big Jim would beat his drum. The only break from dancing was a midnight lunch at the roadhouse. Those of us girls who had danced all night were pretty tired when we got back to Coldfoot. The women had it harder than the men because there weren't enough of them to go around, and they didn't get many chances to rest between dances.

At Christmas we had a big tree in the Pioneers' Hall, and everybody took their presents there. Santa Claus came, in the person of Jim Kelly. In 1934 he had a tame little bull caribou calf with a dog pack filled with toys.

The miners loved children and couldn't give them enough. They were always buying the children bags of peanuts which had to be roasted first or the kids would get sick. Real oranges were a great treat. We ate them, peelings and all. With apples we ate all but the stem. Apples today must be waxed or something. They look too shiny, not like they did years ago. The apples arrived by barge in the fall and were saved in a cool place in the store until Christmas.

One large tree served the whole village. The children decorated it with popcorn strings and real candles. Everything was magic. We sang carols in the Pioneers' Hall, and then carried our gifts home in a pillowcase.

We used to send an order in April to Sears Roebuck or Montgomery Ward by dog team to Tanana. Then it went to Nenana and on to Seward by railroad and by boat to Seattle. Our order arrived around the first of July by the first boat. That order had to last for a year. If anyone made a mistake on the order, he would have to trade or sell to someone. In a few cases, the people had to return items, and Sears would honor an order even a year old.

The arrival of an order was a great time. Sometimes it contained Christmas items which we had to put away for six months. We could always buy from the local trading post, but it didn't carry much variety in goods or supplies, such as yarn. We did a lot of knitting during the long winters, patched our clothing, and darned our socks. When someone was going to have a baby, everyone donated their 50-pound flour sacks for diapers. We washed out the labels with lye soap until the sacks were snowy white. We certainly didn't waste anything.

Even though we were living in the Arctic, we lived out of doors as much as possible. We would start cooking on Friday so we could be free to do other things on Saturday and Sunday. We slept well and ate well with so much exercise. Sometimes we'd light the gas lanterns and hang them near the schoolhouse so we could play soccer ball in the evenings. Even my mother would be out

Joe Ulen and daughter Florence pose with the first
Model T Ford to come to Wiseman. The truck was
brought in by scow in the early 1930s.
(Courtesy of Tishu Ulen)

there playing. Other times whole families would take long walks. And there were always stories to be told to the little ones along the way.

Much of what we did was what you'd call a team effort. If someone on the creeks got sick and called into town for help, we would go out on snowshoes to break trail for the sled. Sometimes 10 of us would stand in line, rotating; when whoever was in the lead tired, the next would take over. It was hard work!

The graveyard at Wiseman was located about a quarter of a mile in back of town. When someone died, we worked together. While two or three men would be making the coffin, others worked in shifts to dig the grave . . . not easy when ground had to be thawed. It was worst in summertime, when they had to get the body into the ground quickly.

When a Catholic died in our town, Pat Keller came from Gold Creek, 25 miles away, to hold services. Pat must have studied to be a priest, because he was able to do a whole service in Latin. It was beautiful, but we couldn't understand a word. I remember the wake for Harry Foley. Mrs. Marson and I put a whole moose ham in the oven at 6:00 A.M. and cooked it all day to make sandwiches for the wake. The whole town ate and danced until 4:00 A.M. After that people took turns sitting up with the body. I guess they did that because Harry was Irish. They did the same for Jack Rafferty. We women baked bread for sandwiches and made dishpans of salad for all who came to pay respects.

Martin Slisco, a Catholic, sent for a priest from Fairbanks to baptize his three children. The ceremony was held in the roadhouse. I remember watching the priest struggling into his cassock and getting his head stuck in his sleeve. Then he ordered candleholders, and Martin didn't have any

Louis Carpenter, early miner on the Koyukuk, climbs the ladder to his cache near Wiseman.
(Courtesy of William English, Jr.)

so he supplied the priest with one Seagram and one Canadian Club bottle. A long mass was held for the houseful of Catholics present. When it was over, the priest asked if anyone would like to confess. Nobody made a move. After lunch the priest invited anyone who would like to confess to come into the kitchen, but still no one moved. I said, "If these people start confessing, you'll be here all summer."

Food was everywhere for anyone who made the effort to get it. We ate a lot of meat — moose, caribou, sheep, rabbit — and the rivers and lakes supplied grayling, trout, pike, whitefish, and an occasional salmon. What we were really most hungry for was vegetables.

I always raised my own vegetables in Wiseman. I started my seeds in April for cabbage, celery, tomatoes, and cucumbers. I kept a fire going at night in my little greenhouse. About May 12 we planted our potatoes in the ground. Carrots went in next along with the cabbage, lettuce, turnips, and radishes. By late June we were eating out of the garden.

When the first turnips were up, we'd boil the tops and eat them and drink the juice. Radish tops went into a salad. How we craved green stuff after the long winters! Everything grows like crazy under the midnight sun, and we tried to help nature along with horse manure and mulch from rotten leaves in the woods.

Every cabin had its own root cellar under the house for storage of vegetables and berries. A good root cellar kept an even, cool temperature all year-round. Meat and fish were kept in a cache outside. We usually put a glaze of ice over the meat to keep it from drying out.

In early summer we were eating fruits, fresh rhubarb, and wild berries. Salmonberries came in June. After salmonberries we'd pick blueberries, which we packed in barrels in the cellar with layers of sugar to preserve them. We'd eat blueberries with canned milk. In July the hills were red with currants, which had to be made into jelly quickly.

After the first frost and just before snowfall, we picked our lowbush cranberries. These kept well in a cache outside through the winter. Picking berries was fun, but we had to look out for black and brown bears. We always took a dog along for protection, but I was never bothered by a bear while berry-picking. I guess our bears were too busy eating.

We had cold, clear water from a spring nearby or from the Koyukuk itself, which had open patches during the winter. Old-timers liked to chip out big ice blocks, which they carried to their cabins and melted slowly for drinking water.

Some winters we had temperatures from 50° to 65° below zero for a time. Every crack in the cabin would let in cold air, so every fall we gathered moss and mixed it with clay, ashes, and moose hair to stuff in spaces between the logs. In the summer temperatures would reach the 80s, and mosquitoes were so bad we couldn't go outside without hat and gloves. Some of the old-timers didn't seem to be bothered by mosquitoes, but they bothered me something terrible. One time Mrs. Jonas and I went down to Moose Creek to fish and had to stop every so often to build a fire and burn off the mosquitoes.

We chopped wood all year. We burned birch and spruce, both green and dry wood. Green logs were used to hold the fire through the night. I saw a few cabins burn down. Albert Ness lost his house because of a chimney fire, so I was careful to pound my stove pipes to keep creosote from forming. When a cabin burned, you had to stay away to avoid shells that might explode.

Sourdough for pancakes and bread was another important part of our lives. We all protected our sourdough pots with as even a temperature as possible. I remember one old man who had had his sourdough pot for many years. When he got sick, he refused to go to the hospital. His neighbors finally found out that he was afraid he'd lose his sourdough. When they offered to keep his sourdough pot going, he went off to the hospital. That same sourdough is still going on. It had been

started with water, sugar, salt, flour, and just a little yeast. You have to work with it, but sourdough gets better as it goes along if you keep using it. I have heard of people who kept their sourdough in bed with them at night for even warmth.

Our Model T was the first pickup in town. It came up by scow in the 1930s. In 1941 we got a Chevy pickup from Frank Pollack. It was flown in dismantled and was welded together at the airport by a mechanic. Some of the people had never ridden in a truck, so it was quite an occasion when it was first driven into town. Soon our 15-year-old Mary was driving all over, and then Florence and Benny. Benny was so short we had to put a pillow under him so he could see through the windshield. There were less than 20 miles of road in the whole Koyukuk River area, and some of it was pretty rough driving.

Joe's Radio

The coming of radio brought the first big change to the Koyukuk. Suddenly the world grew smaller. Joe Ulen came to Bettles in the fall of 1923 and then went on to Wiseman. He was sent by the Army Signal Corps to get needed information for weather and to send messages for the people on the creeks. The Weather Bureau had him record temperatures and wind movements. The Pioneers fixed up a house for Joe, complete with radio pole made from a tall tree. Joe sent his information by Morse code to Tanana, Barrow, and Fairbanks. He worked seven days a week, and he never took a vacation. During World War II, he was up at 4:00 A.M. for his hourly schedule that lasted until 5:00 P.M. In later years he got a radiophone.

Joe and I were married on February 10, 1924, by

This gray jay has found the perfect perch, atop miner Bobby Jones's head, while he stands outside his cabin at Nolan. (Courtesy of William English, Jr.)

Mrs. Mary English (left), Tishu, and Tishu's children Florence (left) and Mary, stand in front of the Army Signal Corps relay station operated by Tishu's husband, Joe Ulen.
(Courtesy of William English, Jr.)

George Huey, the U.S. commissioner. That marriage lasted 41 years. Our wedding was a secret because we were afraid of the crowd. There weren't many girls in town, and when they got married they had an awful time, sort of a kangaroo court, which was all in fun but still a rough time and often embarrassing. The day we were married Joe invited everyone to a big dinner at Slisco's Roadhouse, but he didn't announce our marriage until the next day. A dance was held in our honor to be followed by a bridal shower, but we stayed at the dance until everyone was too tired to do anything but go home. We got by that one. It was fun trying to outwit everyone.

When the *Nanuk* was frozen in the ice the fall of

1929 over in Siberia, my husband and Captain Morgan at Barrow worked their communications. The best time for radio reception was at 1:00 A.M., so it became my job to sit up and wake my husband in time for the messages. It was a long wait, and then Ben Eielson and his mechanic, Earl Borland, were lost while flying over to the stranded ship. I sat up every night sewing and knitting and wondering what had happened to them. I did so much knitting that winter that I ran out of yarn, so I took socks and unraveled them to make something else. In February we finally heard that Eielson's plane had been found. In the next few days Siberian Eskimos helped dig in the hardpacked snow, and the bodies of Eielson and Borland were found. Those Eskimos in Siberia were very interested to learn about living conditions of the Alaskan Eskimos. When the *Nanuk* finally got under way, we could at last go to bed at night. Most people never realized how many other people were involved in the rescue operations.

Joe picked up the message of the Will Rogers-Wiley Post crash at Barrow in 1935. Captain Morgan at Barrow sent it, and Joe relayed it to Fairbanks where the news was spread to the outside world. Joe acted as a relay station because in those days they couldn't get reception across the Brooks Range between Barrow and Fairbanks. Everything went through Wiseman, and we felt as if we were sitting on top of the world with the news. We used a motor generator for power that had to be charged up once or twice a week. If there was a radio breakdown, Joe had to take the equipment apart and solder the lines. I held the wires for him because I had steady hands.

Joe was our link to the rest of the world from 1923 to 1955. By then, there were stronger facilities between Fairbanks and Barrow. Everybody used to come to the house to listen to the news. We even heard radio broadcasts from London and Japan. We first got Anchorage radio station KFQD and later KFAR from Fairbanks. I was usually so tired by 9:00 P.M. that I couldn't stay up, but KFAR's Tundra Topics gave all the personal news at 9:30 P.M. Most villagers waited up for that program.

In the 1940s, Pan American Airways used our radio beam. My husband had to stay on the radio all day, so I packed his food to him. In appreciation for his long hours, Pan Am sent us a huge box of fresh stuff, which unfortunately arrived by plane frozen solid. We could only use the carrots and celery, which I cooked in boiling water.

Whenever there was an emergency, Joe would get on the radio for help. During May no planes could land because of water on the field. I don't remember that anything serious ever went wrong at that time either. Sometimes, when a plane was coming in and the snow had built up on the runway, we would all go out and tromp the runway with our snowshoes. We'd get Jack Hood to help because he weighed 200 pounds. Soon the runway was like a postage stamp.

I used to listen to the radio while working at home. All the pilots were going in different directions, and my job was to keep tabs on them on a map. I remember early one spring hearing Sam White report that he had run out of gas and landed on a river bar between Nenana and Fairbanks. I ran to tell Joe exactly what I'd heard. When Sam was picked up by Noel Wien, Sam wanted to know how Noel found him so fast. When told word came from Wiseman, Sam laughed and said, "Oh, that Mrs. Ulen!" That was fun.

In 1943, just after pilot Herm Joslyn had left Wiseman, an emergency call came for him to land in Livengood and pick up a fellow who had lost his thumb in an accident with a bandsaw. A little after that came another emergency call — from Circle Hot Springs. Owner Johnny Berdahl had had a heart attack and had to get to Fairbanks. Joe contacted Joslyn by radio and told him to stop at Circle Hot Springs. When Joslyn asked Joe how he got his information, Joe said his wife listened to the radio. Sometimes it was hard for me to leave the house with so much news going on in the world. The old-time pilots were all our friends and knew they could depend on us to give them the information they needed while in the air.

Our house was a message center. As our daughters Mary and Florence were growing up, they began carrying messages to people at Hammond River. The girls used to each hook up three dogs and drive the miles to the camp on skis. They always traveled together, sometimes making the round trip in an hour and a half. Later on they would drive the pickup. Joe's radio was a family affair. The pilots called me "Mom" and Joe was "Pop."

The Flying Koyukuk

In early May 1925 a great event took place in the Koyukuk. My husband Joe got word by radio that an airplane was coming in from Fairbanks, flown by Noel Wien and carrying Harper Workman of Nolan Creek and a Mrs. Wheeler. It would be the first airplane to land at Wiseman and above the Arctic Circle.

We were all excited because none of us had ever seen an airplane. Joe told me to tell all the people in town, and he sent word to Hammond and Nolan by battery phone. We waited four hours, standing around the store building and looking down the valley. Suddenly Martin Slisco shouted, "I see it, I see it!" We looked and looked. It was like a fly, but it got bigger. When it got overhead we were all looking up and tried to follow the plane as it circled. I got knocked down three times. Poor Mrs. Big Jim! She was so scared she crawled into a corner of a lean-to and huddled up, shaking from head to foot. I was afraid she'd have a heart attack.

The Standard's wheels touched down safely on a river bar almost in front of the roadhouse. We all rushed down close. The slough water had backed up, but we all jumped in and got our feet wet. Jimmy Tobuk and I were the first to get to the plane.

The passengers sat in an open cockpit in front of the pilot. Mr. Workman had to be helped out because he had a bum leg, and Mrs. Wheeler's long hair was all over the place from streaming out in the wind. We waited until Noel Wien went up to the roadhouse to eat, and then we looked the airplane over carefully.

Noel was a big hero. He was taken over to the Pioneers' Hall and made an honorary member of Igloo #8. After visiting with the people, he refueled, and we all went down to see him off for Fairbanks. We talked about Noel and the plane for days afterward.

After Noel's landing, changes came faster. My

Sig Wien stands next to his Cessna 195 on the Wiseman airstrip. In 1925, Sig's brother Noel made the first flight to land north of the Arctic Circle, stopping at Wiseman. (Courtesy of Shirley English)

first airplane ride was that same summer, 1925. I rode from Bettles to Wiseman with my baby, Mary, in an open Jenny piloted by Joe Crosson. You'd have to get down low out of the wind in the open cockpit but also try to look around a bit. My mother went too. She was so tense she decided she would have to relax a little or she wouldn't last long.

After that summer there were quite a few airplanes. Most flights were made at night in summer when the wind wasn't too strong. The first airstrip at Wiseman was built that summer, but it was always muddy. The road commission workers built a new field in the 1930s, and a crew was stationed there to keep it brushed out in summer. At Old Bettles we still had to take off and land on a river bar. Finally in the 1940s, Bettles Field was built about five miles upstream, and Andy Anderson served as Wien bush pilot, station manager, and hotel operator.

Early pilots into Wiseman after Noel were A.A. Bennett, Joe Crosson, Ed Young, Maurice King, Herm Joslyn, and Frank Pollack. Lon Brennan cracked up on the Wiseman strip. With a lot of freight piled behind him, he really got it. My Florence and Henry Hope pulled him out of the airplane, and he was weaving around with a big bump on his head. Finally he sat down and told us that he felt like a feather when Florence and Henry jerked him out of the cockpit. "Boy, those kids are strong," he said. They worked fast because we were all afraid of fire.

There was something fascinating about airplanes, especially for children. One time Noel Wien and his brother Sig came to town in a Ford

Recently retired as a pilot for Wien Air Alaska, Bill English, Jr., displays an affinity for his future career as he shows his friend Oscar Jonas his first airplane. In the background stand Tishu's house and the old Pioneer Hall at Wiseman.
(Courtesy of William English, Jr.)

Tri-Motor. My daughters, Mary and Florence, and Alice Tobuk climbed in the back and hid. They were around 9 or 10, I guess. When we missed them, it was too late. They were on their way to Fairbanks. I didn't worry though. They told us later they wanted to go to Fairbanks to eat ice cream. They stayed in Fairbanks for five days, ate ice cream, and had a grand time. They were the first stowaways on a plane in Alaska. That story hit the news all over the states.

A few years later my five-year-old Benny climbed into Noel's Tri-Motor in Wiseman. I had to drag him out. Then I got to talking with someone, and the plane started moving. Before we knew it, he too was on his way to Fairbanks, and that was the beginning of his airline career. I'll never know how he got back into the plane. But he had a grand time and came home with a lot of toys. He was sound asleep when Noel brought him home.

During World War II, with many planes overhead, Joe stayed on duty with the radio almost constantly. Navy planes often landed to gas up. Pan Am and Wien brought in the gas. One time a navy plane flipped over on our strip. The pilot was hanging on his belt unconscious. Someone yelled, "Kick the door in!" We kicked it in and dragged the pilot out. Gas was running all over when the pilot woke up and said there were some big shells in the plane. We got out of there in a hurry but, luckily, nothing exploded.

One time a big twin-engine plane landed that needed gas. The pilot needed a funnel and a chamois skin to strain the gas. I told him our chamois skin had holes in it, but if he'd take me home, I'd sew it up in about 20 minutes. I did, and the plane took off for Barrow. We always tried to help the people coming through. Sometimes the pilots came to the house for a bite to eat. And often I heated their oil on my stove in winter and sent them on their way. It was hard not to worry about them at times.

I'll never forget Christmas Eve 1952. I left Fairbanks for Wiseman with Dick McIntyre as pilot. The farther north we went, the deeper we got into fog. We went as far as Gold Creek, and then started down the Koyukuk under the fog. There's a long stretch there and we had to watch out for the trolley, a cage across the river which was run by a cable. I looked out and saw some open water. We were only about five feet above it. Dick landed the plane on the ice, and we got out and looked around before it got too dark. We were only about four miles from Wiseman, and I wanted to go on home, get the dogs, a sleeping bag, and tent. Because the snow was deep, Dick said, "No." I told him we'd better make camp quickly, before dark, with what we had. I cleared snow away from the ground and spread spruce boughs. We made a big fire on the bank. But soon the temperature began to drop rapidly. We put the sleeping bag around the airplane cowling to keep the plane from freezing up, and Dick ran the airplane every hour throughout the night.

It was the longest night of my life, but it was hardest on Dick, who wasn't used to such cold. We ate a bit of food I had brought from Fairbanks, and I lay down by the fire on the new clothing I had bought for my husband. About midnight Dick went out to chop wood for the fire. He came back saying, "I lost the ax." I told him to go back and think which way it had gone when he chopped. He found it, but if he hadn't we would have had to start walking right away. By then it was 40° below. I was glad I had on my fur parky for traveling. Even by the fire, one side freezes while the other burns up when it is that cold.

The skies cleared, and we got into Wiseman at daybreak on Christmas Day. My husband had had a bad night too. He had called everybody on the radio. Some Eskimos said they heard the plane going up Gold Creek. You can hear for miles in that still air. We came through pretty well. Only the tops of my eggs and apples were frozen, and we ate them anyhow. I was sure glad to be home.

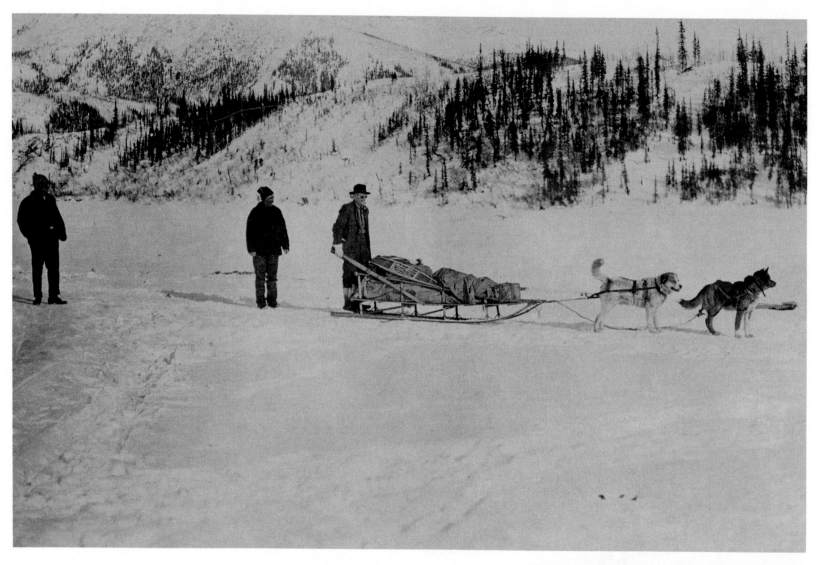

Miners came from all over the world to prospect in the upper Koyukuk. Pete Radicovich (left) and Tom Kovich, both from Yugoslavia, watch as George Eaton guides the sled on a trip out from Wiseman. (Courtesy of Tishu Ulen)

Dog Teams, Trapping, and Sewing

Old-time Eskimo women didn't usually hunt or trap. I guess I took after my father. I did quite a bit of hunting and made good money trapping for many years. In fact, I sent my son out to high school from my trapping money. I would get lynx, fox, wolverine, and wolf pelts. A St. Louis fur buyer usually took my furs, but I did make a lynx coat for my son and often kept wolf pelts for ruffs and parkys. Of course, I also had to keep my snarelines going for dog food, and for rabbit stew from time to time.

I used five dogs for my trapline. In the fall of the year we'd cut the dogs' toenails to keep their feet from getting sore and swollen. Then we'd start hardening them every day with a little work. I used to take my dogs up to Big Lake for two or three weeks of trout fishing in the fall. The 30-mile trip took about eight hours by trail from Wiseman. The rest of the winter, while trapping, I ran my dogs about 20 miles a day.

My trapline started about six miles from Wiseman and ran up Jennie Creek. I would check my traps every five days. I left at 6:00 A.M. and would get back about 4:00 P.M., taking advantage of as much daylight as possible. I was never afraid to be out there alone.

My team ate well when they were working. I fed them each half a rabbit in the morning and cooked food late in the afternoon. I would cook oats and melt tallow, which was poured over the oats. The hard, rendered beef tallow came in 50-pound cans from the store. To have a good team you have to feed it well. In the summer the dogs ate lighter, but they needed a lot of water. They seemed to be happy when winter came because they liked to get on the trail and pull. Each dog had its own box house built two feet off the ground with shelter underneath for summer. Inside each house was plenty of fresh, dry hay gathered in the fall. All dogs were fastened to their houses by a five-foot chain.

I often traveled between Wiseman and Bettles in one day with a fast trail. There was a roadhouse at Coldfoot and another at Roy King's fox farm. I always carried my own dog food, and the dogs ate snow for water. I used to take a shortcut across the hills rather than following the winding river all the way. That trail is still there and can be seen from the air.

I was proud of my team. Two of the dogs had some Saint Bernard in them. They had huge long legs. Their dispositions were so good they could eat together and never growl. Three of my dogs lived to be 14 years old, and could still run. It all depends on how well you take care of them.

Lippy, my leader, was smart and fast. Silver-gray and beautiful, she was a one-person dog, probably because she was part wolf. She watched me all the time. She would mate with only one dog and was deathly afraid of wolves. Because I had raised her, she trusted me to handle her pups, but no one else could touch them. Those pups were always in demand because of the wolf strain. I never knew a dog so quick to respond. If I wanted her to take out on a fast run, all I had to do was tap the sled and she'd go for miles.

I guess Lippy was special to me because she saved our lives once. She was leading six dogs across the ice at Big Lake one spring. I was driving with Florence and Benny in the sled. Suddenly I saw the water start bubbling up, and the ice began to sag. I was too frightened to say anything. But I grabbed my fishpole and hit the sled. Lippy took off like a shot just before the ice caved in. We would have sunk in that icy water and couldn't have lasted long. When we got to shore, I just held Lippy and talked to her for a long time. I told her how much I loved her, and she knew it.

Later Lippy got distemper when Bobby Jones brought in a dog from Fairbanks. I lost her three puppies, and Lippy never got well. For a year I fed her by hand. During the summer she seemed to get worse, and my husband said she was suffering.

Finally I had to give her up though I wanted to keep her always. When I came home to her empty box, I felt terrible.

We called my half-coyote Tiger, but he was a timid and gentle little thing that never growled or got in a fight. He worked hard and seemed to be smart. He was mostly black with white spots. One morning when I went out to feed him, I couldn't find his box. It had snowed heavily in the night, and I had to poke around with a stick until I found him. His cute little head came out. He seemed to be glad I'd found him under the snow.

My dogs enjoyed the trapline. They liked going out, but they also liked coming home because they knew they'd have a good feed. One winter I had a bad sinus attack while on the trapline. I could hardly see because of the pain, so I sat down on the sled with my mitt over my face. I let the dogs go, and they brought me safely home. I could depend on my team.

I saw wolf tracks near my line one spring. The tracks were small and away from my trail so I set my trap out there. One morning I came out and the willows were moving. I knew there was a wolf in there. The dogs always acted funny with a wolf around. I tied my dogs and took my .22 rifle up close. The wolf saw me, put her head up high, and howled an almost human cry. It was deep and gave me goose bumps all over. I stood there and she howled again. I still stood there. She howled a third time. Then she turned and started chewing willows, and the minute she turned I shot her. I had to do it quickly. I guess she was calling her mate. There was no answer. It was frightening.

You hear stories about how fierce a wolf can be. Arctic Johnnie told me a story about a pack of 40 wolves. He shot one and wounded it. The rest of the wolves broke trail for the wounded one. They even killed a caribou to bring him meat. Johnnie followed the trail of that wounded wolf for a week, but he never caught up with it. Each day it gained strength. Through his field glasses Johnnie watched the other wolves surround the wounded one and take turns licking him. With the help of the pack, the wounded one recovered and escaped.

Coyotes came into the country in later years. I never saw one because they stayed away from people, but they yipped out there. We often heard wolf howls not too far away, but no wolves ever attacked our dogs. They could surely get them upset though. I did see a white fox come into Coldfoot one time. The fox was thought to have rabies because it bit Harry Snowden through his felt shoe, but Harry never got sick. Foxes didn't breed with dogs, but wolves and coyotes did now and then.

After I brought the pelts in from the trapline, there was plenty more work to do. I had to clean the animal, scrape the skin, and hang it up overnight where it was warm. When I could run my fingernails on it and it crackled, the skin was ready for tanning. Then I would sit on the floor and take a part of the brain and work it in. When it was wet, I would fold it up for the night. The next day I would start rubbing and scraping it out. Then I could start cutting out whatever I wanted.

My mother taught me to sew skins the way she learned when she was growing up. I would always crease the skin first and then cut on the crease with an *ulu*. Sinew for thread came from the back of a caribou. The blood was cleaned out, the hide scraped thin, then dried, and the sinew split for different types of sewing. A tough piece of hide was used for a thimble in the old days, and bone needles were carved before there were steel needles.

I started learning to sew on caribou socks. Then I went on to men's boots and finally made a parky. To get the right size for boots, I had to look carefully at a person's foot. Then I made the boots an inch longer than foot size, though hunters usually want their caribou socks tight. I never made the hard-soled boots because we lived in the mountains and didn't have sealskin and *oogruk* from the arctic coast. We used bull caribou skin for our soles and in

Tishu, at about age 15, models a parka she made.
(Courtesy of Tishu Ulen)

later years soft moose skin. The upper part was from the skin of caribou legs; we used the thin flank skin for trim at the top until we got colorful felt.

Men always carried a mending outfit of needle and thread when they went hunting. They had to be able to sew a little in case their clothing tore. The men did the hunting and cleaned the game, but the women hauled it in and cut it up. A few women also hunted. My mother taught me to snare rabbits by using sinew tied to a spring pole. The rabbit would go up in the air.

There wasn't much time for making fancy things, but I do remember seeing some designs out of white sheepskin and caribou, decorated with dyes from salmon, blueberries, and bark. With wolverine we used alderwood bark. We'd scrape until we had a nice red color. Red was popular because everyone got so tired of white snow all the time. There were actually many different shades of dyes from berries.

I remember when the old-time Eskimo women wore parkys with fawn skin next to their bodies. They were so warm they could sit on a snowbank and be warm in winter. In the summer they wore lightweight skins. The furs and skins were lovely, but after the trading posts opened at Bettles and Coldfoot, all the women wanted cotton print dresses.

Furs were better than money in most cases. My mother told of when she went to buy a dress, Mrs. Howard at the Coldfoot post said, "One fox skin for one dress." So my daddy went out trapping. The next morning he had a red fox for her. But the other ladies were picking the dresses over pretty fast, and to hurry it up Mama hung her fox skin too close to the heat. When she went to turn it, the hair all fell out. There went her dress. So my father set two more traps, and the next day he got two more foxes. Then she was able to go to the store at Coldfoot and get two dresses. They were long cotton print dresses that came down to her ankles, and she felt she was in style.

My Koyukuk Friends

I grew up hearing languages and accents of people from all over the world. We had a sampling of Yugoslavians, Germans, Irish, French-Canadians, Poles, Greeks, Swedes, Japanese, and Welsh. There was also a mixture of Eskimos from the arctic coast and Kobuk country and a very few Indians. A few of the miners had families waiting for them at home, but most were bachelors. Only a few hardy white women followed their men out to the creeks. Some of the miners took Eskimo wives, so the children in the area were full or part Eskimo. The miners really enjoyed the children.

Every old-timer had a special story to tell of how he came to the Northland, and why he stayed. I never knew Gordon Bettles, one of the very first whites in Koyukuk country before the time of the Klondike gold rush. He left the country before I was born, but the trading post he built around 1899 played a large part in our lives. Bettles, the town staked in 1900 around his post at the mouth of the

John River, was the first real settlement in the upper Koyukuk. Gordon Bettles, his wife, and brother Tom were in and out of Gold Creek on the South Fork, with different mining operations.

My daddy remembered John Nolan when he first started working the ground on Nolan Creek. Daddy was out hunting to bring fresh meat to the store at Coldfoot. Nolan kept telling my daddy to stake some ground, but my daddy only said, "What for?" Gold didn't mean much to him. After the big strike at Nolan, Hammond River came next. Then the settlement at Wiseman Creek began to grow near Wright's Roadhouse and finally became Wiseman.

Carl Frank, a German, came to the country around 1900. He operated a roadhouse down by Tramway Bar, mined on Gold Creek, and then moved up to Wiseman to make his home in his later years. Carl had had a fiancee in Germany, but something happened and Carl left home for good and came to Alaska. He would have made a good husband. He loved to garden and cook and was always clean and neat. He used to sing German

(Right→) *Martin Slisco, who with his cousin Jack mined on Myrtle Creek, also operated a roadhouse at Wiseman.* (Courtesy of Tishu Ulen)

(Opposite→) *Old Bettles, the original townsite platted in 1900 by Gordon C. Bettles, grew to become the major supply point for the upper Koyukuk until lack of a suitable spot to build an airstrip brought about a shift in the community's population to five miles upriver.* (Gil Mull)

songs to us. He never hunted, so we used to bring him meat, and he gave us vegetables from his garden. Like so many of the old-timers who stayed on in the Koyukuk, Carl lived a long life. He was 96 when he died.

Albert Ness was a Swede who went through the 1906 San Francisco earthquake. At that time he was married and had two small children. His home was destroyed. While he and his wife tried to salvage a few belongings, his wife's sister came by and offered to take the girls to safety. But the sister and the girls vanished. They searched and searched. Finally they decided the sister and the girls must have been swallowed up in a crack. Albert eventually went north to Dawson, then returned to get his wife, who never recovered from the loss of her children. She died, and Albert moved on to the Koyukuk. He mined at Hammond awhile, and then spent the rest of his life in Wiseman. He kept a beautiful garden. Albert Ness was a real gentleman. I took care of him one spring after he had a stroke. He lived into his late 80s.

John Bowman was from Switzerland. He made a lot of money on the Hammond River, but he didn't like to live there. He hired people to work for him and only went out to the creek to collect his gold. His greatest talent was spending money, but he never seemed to get beyond Bettles before it was gone. He wanted to make a trip Outside, so his friends decided to help him. They stole his poke of gold while he was drinking in Bettles and saved it for him until he sobered up. He did make his trip but came back broke. He then went out to Lake Iliamna on a mining venture, and while crossing the thin ice in the spring, he fell through and drowned. A week after his death, he received a big inheritance from a relative in Switzerland. I don't know where the money went from there because he had no family in this country.

Quite a few of the miners were from Yugoslavia. They came first to Flat and then into the Koyukuk. They congregated at Porcupine Creek — George and Steve Bojanich, Sam and O'Brien Stanich, Tom Kovich, and Pete Radovich. Martin Slisco was up on Myrtle Creek with his cousin Jack Slisco. Martin also ran the roadhouse in Wiseman. When he wanted a wife he went back to the old country to get a bride. He chose Para, who was very young and pretty. I helped my mother and Mrs. Wilcox deliver her first child. She had a hard time. They had three young children when Martin was shot and killed by Jack Welch in a quarrel. His murderer was sent to jail for life, and Para moved to Fairbanks. The children grew up there, and both boys eventually became dentists.

Mr. and Mrs. Arthur ("Casey") Hill kept a roadhouse, first at Coldfoot and then at Wiseman. Casey loved to work, and he was happy as a lark in Wiseman. His wife insisted that they move to Seattle in 1922, so we held a big farewell dance for the Hills. Just before leaving, Casey baked a lot of bread and delivered a loaf to each house in town. He had made good money with his roadhouse where he served big meals for a dollar. But more than that, Casey made a lot of friends who missed him. He never came back.

Most miners moved on, but those bachelors who stayed had no one to look after them. Old-timer Knute Ellingson struck the first big money in the Koyukuk about 1899. As Knute got up in his 80s, his mind began to wander and he kept dreaming of new gold strikes. One winter day when it was 30° below, he started out walking from his home without mitts. Luckily, Harry Leonard saw him before he got far down the trail and brought him back home. He kept wanting to run off. He'd say, "There's a big stampede on — you better get ready to go." When he came to my house to tell me to get started, I'd give him a bowl of soup. Charlie Irish, the U.S. commissioner, finally stayed with Knute until we could get him sent to the Pioneers' Home at Sitka.

Two Japanese friends were Frank Yasuda and Minnie Minano, who had trekked with their Eskimo

(Left ←) *One of the early finds which attracted miners to the upper Koyukuk occurred on Nolan Creek. Kenneth Harvey (center) and Bobby Jones were partners in a mine along the creek. Harvey also drove a Cat from Wiseman to Bettles hauling freight for the Wiseman Trading Company. In this photo, the two miners pose with their friend, Biner ("Billy") Wind at Nolan Creek.* (Courtesy of William English, Jr.)

(Below ↓) *Harry Leonard steps outside his cabin around his 85th birthday in July 1982. Harry came to the Koyukuk in 1934, making him not only the oldest but also the longest resident now living in Wiseman. Until several years ago, Harry mined on Gold Creek and Nolan Creek.* (Walter Johnson)

(Left ←) *Colorful sourdoughs lived in scattered camps throughout the upper Koyukuk, working the frozen ground in hopes of finding paydirt. Hans Christensen plied his trade at a mine near Big Lake, east of Wiseman.* (Courtesy of William English, Jr.)

Mr. and Mrs. Jacob Jonas stand in front of their cabin in 1972. The Jonas family divided their time between Wiseman and Big Lake, 30 miles to the north. The Jonases had one of the few families that grew up in the Wiseman area.
(Walter Johnson)

wives from the arctic coast to Chandalar and then moved down the rivers to settle in Wiseman and Beaver. I think they had sailed on the whaling ships. Both Yasuda and Minano raised fine families in the Arctic. Yasuda's daughter graduated from the University of Alaska and became a schoolteacher.

Pete Haslin was a proud and stubborn man who didn't want to leave Wiseman and refused all help when he became old. In fact, he suffered from malnutrition in his later years. We had to trick him to get him off to the Pioneers' Home at Sitka. When a plane arrived to pick him up, I suggested that several of us pile into the plane to make him think we were going for a ride. When he was in, we all jumped out quickly. The door was closed, and the plane took off. In Sitka we heard that Pete improved and enjoyed keeping a garden there.

Hughie Boyle was an old Irishman from San Francisco who mined on Nolan Creek. Hughie's claim to fame was his dancing. In fact, we heard he had run a ballroom somewhere Outside. Hughie was the best dancer in town, even when he was in his 80s. He used to sit on the sidelines at the dances

and rub his knees to get the circulation going. Pretty soon he'd be on his feet and would start clapping his hands, and when he finally took to the floor, a Wiseman dance was in full swing. Hughie was in his 90s when he died in his own cabin. He refused all help and wouldn't go in to Fairbanks to the hospital.

The famous biologist Olaus Murie and his brother, Adolph, arrived around 1922. They were the first to study the wildlife of the Koyukuk and the movements of the caribou. They carried animals in little cages. When Olaus came back in 1924, his bride, Margaret, was with him. They mushed up the Koyukuk after freezeup and arrived just in time for a caribou migration through the Brooks Range. It was the first big one in many years through that part of the country. The hills were alive with caribou. I don't know where they go anymore.

Nakuchluk became Big Jim's wife after Peluk disappeared in a hunting accident. She and Big Jim were hospitable and friendly leaders of the Eskimo community. They held prayer meetings in their home. Big Jim drove a team of nine part-wolf dogs on his trapline, and Nakuchluk made parkys, caribou pants, and boots from the furs and skins he brought in. Big Jim usually stayed out alone on the trapline through the winter, coming into town only for Thanksgiving and Christmas. They always served raw fish to their guests. Big Jim's drum added a lot to the dances. After Big Jim died at Big Lake, Nakuchluk stayed on in Wiseman that spring and summer. She even traveled to Fairbanks. After her return from the big city, she told of seeing a naked mannequin in a clothing store there. She was shocked. "The people of Fairbanks are shameless," was her comment.

Only a handful of white women lived in the Koyukuk: a few miners' wives, schoolteachers who usually married after a year or two of teaching, and wives of roadhouse operators such as Mrs. Miller. Mrs. Brooks followed her doctor husband around on the creeks. And of course, there was Mrs. Louisa Pingel, the Episcopal missionary lady who lived with her husband at Nolan Creek. There were sporting girls from time to time. A few of them married miners and became good wives. I never saw much of the sporting girls because Mama made me stay away from them. She said they were "different."

Nellie Cashman was a wonderful person and a lot of fun. She had come over the Chilkoot Pass to Dawson and then down to the Koyukuk. She had many business ventures and traveled around the country alone. When I knew her she was white-haired and past 60, but still plucky and hot-tempered. Whenever she was angry, people would say "Keep your shirt on, Nellie," and that would really get her Irish temper going. On her last trip to Wiseman she became very ill. I nursed her for two weeks until a boat arrived. We never saw Nellie after that, but we never forgot her.

Robert Marshall, author of *Arctic Village*, got along well with the people of Wiseman. He took a lot of pictures and entered into the activities of the town. He must have had a good memory, but he also took down whole conversations in shorthand, which he wrote in the palm of his hand. We didn't know just what he was doing that year, but he was busy.

The day our copies of the book *Arctic Village* arrived, we were getting ready for a dance. I looked at the beautiful pictures, but didn't have time to read the book. When I got to the dance, no one was dancing. I kept hearing, "I thought you were my friend. Why did you say those things about me?" There was a war in Wiseman that night, and no dance. Everyone was too busy arguing. When Marshall came back to Wiseman the following year, I shook his hand and asked him, "Did you come back to listen some more in the keyholes?" I was the first to greet him, then the others took after him. But everything simmered down after awhile. He really was a nice person.

When Marshall came back, he wrote a book about the mountains of the Brooks Range. He took Kenneth Harvey, Jesse Allen, Harry Snowden, an Eskimo boy, and two dogs on an expedition to climb Mount Doonerak. They were gone a long time that summer mapping and exploring in the Brooks, but they never made it to the top of Doonerak.

Bob Marshall renamed Rooney's Lake as Big Lake. John Rooney, from Ireland, first settled on the lake. Whenever we went up to go fishing, Rooney gave us salted trout in barrels. He died up there in the 1940s and was buried across the lake. Big Jim, Jacob Jonas, Fred Terrell, and Charlie Irish gave him a funeral the way Rooney wanted it. We found later that Rooney, who had worked the ground for years, was only a few feet from a good paystreak. He never knew how close he was. Later, Fred Pitts had a great summer on the same ground.

I could go on and on about the many people who came and went in our lives. Those who stayed lived to a ripe old age so they must have had a pretty good life in the Koyukuk. Not many died with much money, but it didn't take much money to live there and be happy.

Only The Mountains Are The Same

Today I have more comfort than I used to have, but I like the old ways best and sometimes I pine for the way it was. There was no waste. We had to make do with a little bit, but we were active and happy and had such good times together. It's hard to grow old and see everything change.

In the old days we never hurried. Life moved by the sun. We didn't need to look at watches. Our work followed the order of the seasons. In the winter we traveled by dog team and trapped and hunted. In the spring we traveled by night when the snow was hard. Then we'd stay in one place until after breakup and the ice was out of the rivers. Summer came fast, and we often stayed up all night fishing or gardening under the midnight sun. In late summer and fall we picked berries, hunted, and prepared our cabins for winter. We were always gathering and chopping wood to keep fires going. We worked hard, but we played hard too. In winter I used to take my kids out to see the sky lit up by red and green northern lights. We'd clap our hands and say "Shhh," a hissing noise, to make the northern lights dance.

There was no smog in the Koyukuk. The air was always clean and clear. At night we'd see wood smoke rising from the cabins. If there wasn't any smoke, it was time to go check on someone. We all looked out for one another.

We had everything we needed — food, wood to burn, fresh air, fresh spring water, and friends. A lot of drinking went on, of course, but we didn't see much of it, we only heard it. There was some stealing of pokes, but most people were honest. We could leave our cabin unlocked without anyone bothering it. Now most of the old-timers are gone, and few people know how it was. Newcomers have taken over the old cabins — pipeline workers, hunting guides, and a few road workers. And a few of us, like myself, like to go back to remember the way it was. But everything changes. Old Wiseman

In the summer of 1982, a smiling Tishu Ulen returned to visit Wiseman. (Sharon English)

has grown up in willows, and even the Koyukuk River has changed its channel. I barely recognize Coldfoot since it has grown into a pipeline haul road stop. Only the mountains are the same.

Sometimes I can't wait to join all my relatives and friends who have gone on. But I guess I'll have to stay here until I don't have anymore work to do. I like to think about climbing my mountains around Wiseman and spending the night up there. I used to watch the sun set across the peaks and it was all so beautiful, I would think I could live forever. I've seen 77 years of change. After my next birthday, I think I'll start going backward.

This plane, cache, and cabin are part of Rick Reakoff's guiding operations at Wiseman. The building was built as a school at Coldfoot about 1915. The cabin was disassembled and moved to Wiseman where it served as a schoolhouse until the school closed in 1941. (Walter Johnson)

(Left ←) *The Slisco roadhouse, shown here in 1972, has since fallen as do most sod-roofed buildings that are without a metal cover.* (Walter Johnson)

(Below ↓) *This placer mine on the South Fork Koyukuk was active until the 1940s.*
(Steve McCutcheon)

(Right →) *Cabins left behind by miners during the rush to the Koyukuk lie nestled in the valley of the Middle Fork Koyukuk near Coldfoot.*
(Steve McCutcheon)

Koyukuk Journal: Window of History

By Shirley English

Excitement was in the spring air of 1902 in the upper Koyukuk country. As the frenzied gold rush to the Klondike waned, the word was out of good prospects along the upper Koyukuk River. Many miners had left Dawson by dog team the previous winter, traveling down the frozen Yukon and up the Chandalar River toward Slate Creek and other diggings. Gordon Bettles' trading post was becoming a focal point for supplies and river traffic. Some hardy souls reached the Koyukuk from the Yukon via the Dall River trail, and others arrived by steamboat after breakup, filtering upstream from Saint Michael or Koyukuk Station through Bergman to Bettles, the head of navigation. Poling boats and horse-drawn scows completed the long journey over shallows and riffles to the creeks. Some 70 river miles upstream from Bettles was the burgeoning mining community of Coldfoot.

On March 1, 1902, someone began keeping a detailed journal at Bettles. The journal entries, written in ink with a fine hand, were made on a daily basis in a book used originally as a hotel register in Bennett, British Columbia, in 1899. How this book reached Bettles and whose hand made the entries may always remain mysteries. But the journal is a factual record of the origins and destinations of all who passed through Bettles. Trail conditions and weather were duly noted, as were arrivals of mail carriers and steamboats. Through the eyes of the journal writer, a bygone era is alive with details of events, altercations, and tragedies of those who played a part in Alaska history.

Many of the communities mentioned in the journal have vanished without a trace, their lives too brief to be fixed on a map. Who today has every heard of Kelly's Mistake, Shamrock City, or Hot Foot? Old Bettles itself crumbled into memories, to be replaced by modern Bettles Field, five miles upriver. Coldfoot, a ghost town, was reborn as an Alyeska Pipeline camp in the 1970s.

The color and humor of the Alaska gold rush can be seen in the nicknames or pseudonyms used by some of the travelers. There were Tommy Wooden Shoes, Silent Willie, Tupper Thompson, Mukluk Jack, Smiling Albert, Handsome Harry, Hungry Bill, Flap Jack Louis, Kangaroo Kelly, and the irrepressible Argo Bill. Moving through the pages of this journal are also such names as Gordon Bettles and his family, pre-gold rush pioneers; John Nolan, discoverer of rich Nolan Creek; J. Wada, who was soon to play a part in the rush to Fairbanks; August Tobin, longtime miner whose son established *The ALASKA SPORTSMAN®* magazine; and, of course, Volney Richmond, manager of Northern Commercial Company.

When the N.C. Company bought the two-story log trading post of Pickarts, Bettles, and Pickarts, young Volney Richmond was given his first assignment there. He quickly established a branch store at Coldfoot with Bob Menzie in charge. Richmond worked hard and traveled constantly to supply the many mining camps springing up on creeks of the Middle and South forks of the Koyukuk. Although highly respected by the miners, Richmond's run-in with Argo Bill caused a stir that reverberated through the camps, judging by the following entries:

4/1/02: *Argo Bill made a demand from Richmond of the N.C. Co. for meat he had left at the warehouse, which was refused him. Henceforth gun play by Argo Bill. Bill got the meat.*

4/13/02: *Argo Bill was arrested, charged with assault with a deadly weapon upon Richmond of the N.C. Co.*

4/23/02: *Judge McKenzie and attorney Salsberry had a fistic contest at Coldfoot in which his honor was knocked out in one round. This set-to was caused over a controversy between principals in the Argo Bill case. The attorney was arrested and put in jail for two hours when the judge russelled bond for the prisoner. Bond $500.*

4/30/02: *Wm. Henderson (Argo Bill) was discharged. Prosecuting witness (Richmond) failing to put in his appearance at the trial.*

The story finally concluded with the following note:

5/4/02: *Richmond reports that Judge McKenzie assessed him $5.00 and costs for contempt of court for not appearing in the Argo Bill case . . . the total amounting to $318. Richmond appealed the case.*

A bulletin from Coldfoot in May gave a brief summary of events there:

5/20/02: *Billy Devine broke Jim Graham's jaw in a fight. Devine was arrested and fined $25 and costs. Gowans stole a poke from Vern Casley containing $87. Gowans was arrested and lodged in jail.*
Jim Graham presented Maud with a pair of black eyes. Big strike reported on Hammond and Vermont Creek. W.J. Daily (Red) stabbed Wm. Carroll across the breast. Red is in jail, Carroll is getting along nicely. Dr. Cleveland put in 21 stitches.

Many important events were recorded on the pages of this journal, kept at Bettles in the early 1900s. This page shows the results of the census taken on August 7, 1902, and duly reports the completion of the pool table and exact hour at which the first game of pool to be played in Bettles began.
(Polly Walter, staff)

Hotel register page (August 1902):

HOTEL REGISTER.
Money, Jewelry and other Valuables must be placed in the Safe in the Office, otherwise the Hotel will not be responsible for any loss.

DATE	NAME	RESIDENCE	ROOM	TIME OF ARRIVAL

Tuesday 5th — John Bowman — arr. from Coldfoot
Flap Jack Louis
The Pool Table was finished at 10:30 P.M. and the first game of pool played in the city was played at the above hour.

Wednesday 6th — Phil Vincent — left for Coldfoot
Gus Lessing

Thursday 7th — Total Number of People residing in Bettles at this date — 49 —
31 White Men, 8 White Women, 2 Indians, 4 Squaws, 4 Indian Kids

V. Richmond — Olsen — Mrs. Grimm
J. Sellars — Crocker — " Place
Ch. Grimm — Flemming — " Dahms
Tom Hulbert — J. Baird — " G. Bettles
Geo. L. Rice — Victor Beifield — " J.
Simon Hirsch — Alex Hollenberg — " Flowers
Frank Gauta — L. Traxler — Miss Stevens
Ch. Mathews — A.K. Amero — " Millie Jackson
Bob Bingham — Manuel Lewis — 2 Indian Men
Rush — J. Bowman — 4 " Women
Albert Lind (Chinling) — Albert J. Flowers — 4 " Kids
H.C. Henshaw — K. Dians
Wm. McNeil — J.G. Pickhants
K. Haugh
O.M. Manzar (Ling)
P. Mahoney
Barber
Napoleon Dubras

103

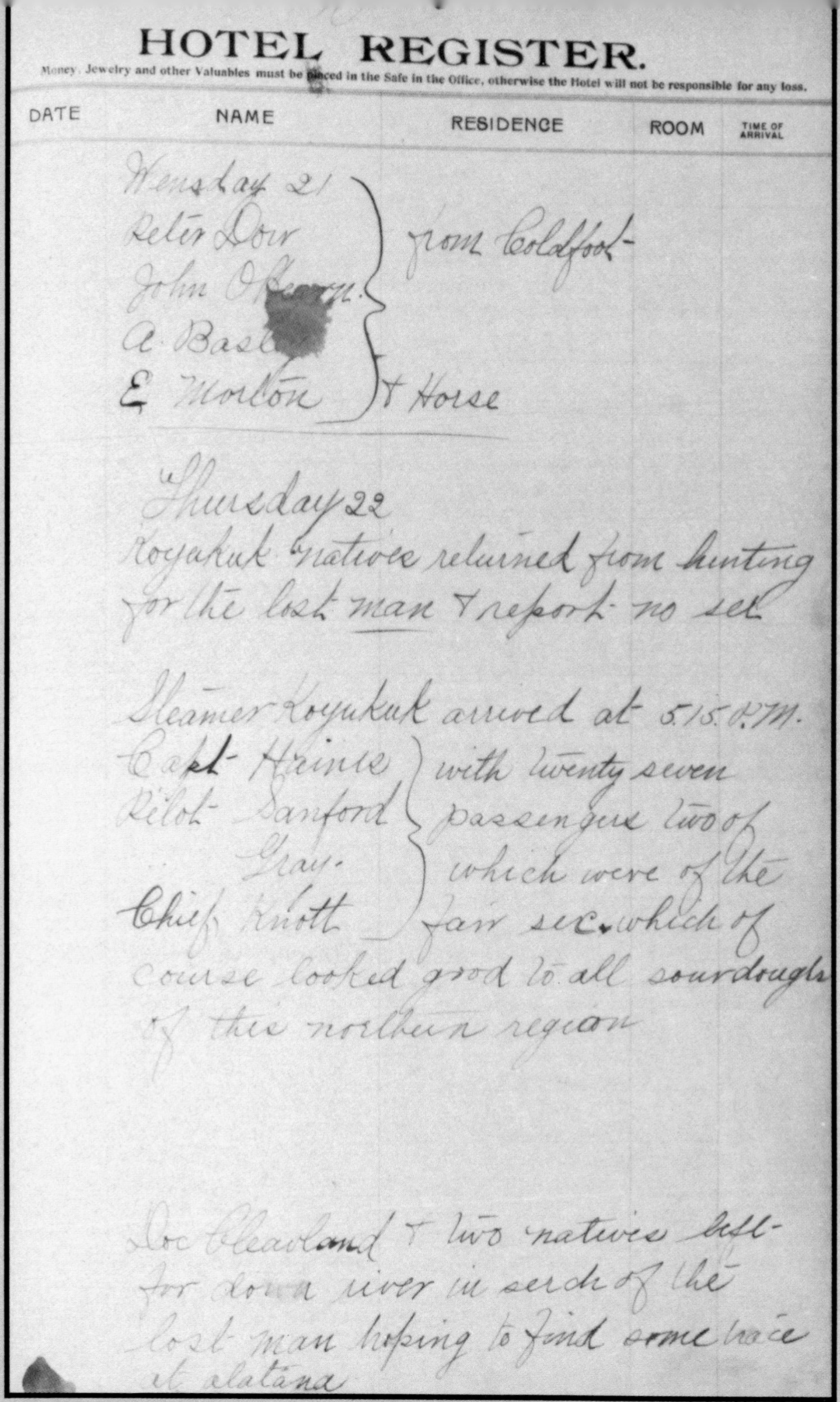

HOTEL REGISTER.

Money, Jewelry and other Valuables must be placed in the Safe in the Office, otherwise the Hotel will not be responsible for any loss.

DATE	NAME	RESIDENCE	ROOM	TIME OF ARRIVAL

Wensday 21
Peter Dow ⎫
John O'Berry ⎬ from Coldfoot
A Basl ⎪
E Morton ⎭ & Horse

Thursday 22
Koyukuk natives returned from hunting for the lost man & report no sell

Steamer Koyukuk arrived at 5.15 P.M.
Capt Hines ⎫ with twenty seven
Pilot Sanford ⎬ passengers two of
      Gray ⎪ which were of the
Chief Knott ⎭ fair sex. which of
course looked good to all sourdoughs
of this northern region

Doc Cleavland & two natives left
for down river in serch of the
lost man hoping to find some trace
at alatana

In the optimistic climate of Bettles, free enterprise began to flourish. For example:

5/15/02: *Jim Baird has located the Paystreak in Bettles. He opened up the claim last Saturday, and it is showing up good. He is fanning out and cleaning up each day . . . in other words he is making the Big Raise of the Dough.*

The Paystreak, a restaurant and bakery, lasted only until December 15 of the same year, when Baird got off his Paystreak. Other ventures were the French Scurvy Cure Company of Napeau and Lucy, which made its appearance at Bettles and Coldfoot and then moved on to greener pastures in Nome, and the first edition of *The North Pole*, a spicy newspaper on blue print which enlivened folks up and down the river.

When there were problems, the miners recognized the strength in unity and worked together to solve their problems. An example from the journal is:

10/2/02: *The following citizens constructed a new bridge over the Gulch today, which is a very creditable job . . . Martin Christenson, Olsen, Ernest Bier Brown, Roberts, Mike McNeal, Charley Pickarts, Barber, Chas. Matthews, P.M. Manzar, and Hirsch. The N.C. Co. furnished nails and 2x3 lumber for railing. Pickart Bettles & Pickart furnished the slabs, and a lunch was given by James Baird, the N.C. Co. contributing crackers, cheese, and sardines.*

In the eventful summer of 1902 a sad accident

Sandwiched between entries concerning a search for a lost man comes the news of the arrival of the steamer Koyukuk on June 22, 1903, with two women among the passengers. The missing man was found, apparently in good health, a few days later. (Polly Walter, staff)

took place on the trail between Bettles and Coldfoot. Excerpts from the journal tell the story:

7/1/02: Burt Barton while on his way to Coldfoot was drowned this morning about 9:30 in the Koyukuk River at the mouth of John River. Deceased was 23 years old last April. He leaves his father (in this town) to mourn his loss . . . Deceased was very popular, a bright young man and of good qualities. Dr. Cleveland's eyewitness statement: Dr. Cleveland and others left here this morning for Coldfoot with a scow loaded with freight. Burt was driving one of the mules in crossing the mouth of the John River. Burt was swimming with the lines in hand, in some unaccountable manner he lost his hold, perhaps frightened by the mule being swept under the water . . . As he was trying to gain the shore, he suddenly disappeared under the water and never was seen after that.

Frank Howard found Barton's body a mile above Peavy on July 17. Frank Banta, Joe Rasperson, Roy Reed, Al Thompson, and Sam Barton, the father, went downriver to Peavy, where burial took place.

Another journal entry is the following:

9/28/02: Barber Andrews was arrested for being implicated in stealing a poke worth $300 from Rooney at Coldfoot.

Andrews' grief must have been great, for he committed suicide two days later by "tying a rock around his neck and jumping into the Koyukuk River in front of Coldfoot."

A census was taken of Bettles in August 1902. It revealed the names of "31 white men, 8 women, 2 Indian men, 4 Indian women, and 4 kids" with a total of 49 people residing in Bettles. Among other statistics listed were:

The Koyukuk River closed at Bettles on October 6, 1901. The coldest day in the winter of 1901-1902 was -78 degrees in January. Ice started moving in the Koyukuk at 4:43 P.M. on May 15, 1902.

An ice pool had been formed, but since only four guesses were accumulated at a dollar a guess, the money was refunded and the pool declared off. The failure was "attributed to the stringency in the money market."

Spring breakup on the Koyukuk was dramatic, judging by the following account:

5/23/03: Ice started to move between here and John River at 8 A.M. The Nina broke her line and is out in the ice about 300 feet above the store. Got another line to her. Ice moved in front of town at 3:15 P.M. and stopped at 3:25 P.M. Saved the Nina by pulling her out and beaching her below Napoleon's Saloon. The water is within 12 inches of the top of the banks at 5:00 P.M. Water coming over the banks into the street.

5/24/03: The ice jam broke at 8:50 P.M. About 6 inches of water in front of the saloon, had a boat afloat. At 10:30 P.M. the river is clear of ice.

And so the ice came and went, as did the people. A few found gold in paying quantities and some left the country broke. Some moved on to the beaches of Nome, while others headed for the new gold camp of Fairbanks in the Tanana Valley. And some of the names that were prominent in the journal became sourdoughs in Wiseman, which was soon to become a center of mining for the entire Koyukuk country. A new hand took over the journal in 1903, but the attention to detail and sense of drama spiced with humor are missing. The journal came into the hands of U.S. Commissioner George Huey, who eventually passed the book on to Joe and Tishu Ulen at the village of Wiseman. The book is now one of Tishu's priceless possessions, a window of Koyukuk history and an endless source of information concerning Koyukuk pioneers.

105

Wiseman, Then and Now

By Walter Johnson

Editor's note: *Walter Johnson came to Alaska in 1941, and made his home in Wiseman off and on during the next four decades. He was a practicing physician for many years and is presently coordinator of community health aide training for the Division of Rural Education at the University of Alaska, Anchorage.*

Fifty years ago, Alaska was dotted with small mining towns. With few exceptions, they are gone. Several have grown into cities, but most of them have disappeared from the list of Alaska post office addresses. Many of the small mining communities have fallen into ruin and decay with only rotting logs, rusting metal, and changes in the vegetation pattern to mark their sites.

Wiseman is one of the few early mining camps that has survived. Although mining in the Wiseman area declined during World War II, it has never completely ceased. Today not all of Wiseman's few permanent residents still mine, but the airstrip, roads, and trails act as a center for prospectors and small mining operators still in existence.

Wiseman was never a big camp like Nome or Fairbanks. In its more prosperous days in the early 1900s, several hundred people lived in the Wiseman area. By the 1930s the population had declined, and World War II almost spoke the death knell.

When I first visited Wiseman in the early 1940s, there were only a couple dozen people living in the village and surrounding area. The school had closed just before the war. At the beginning of World War II all of the young people left for construction jobs, to enter the service, or to attend school. During the war, the average age of the residents of Wiseman climbed to about 65. This included such residents as Hughie Boyle, in his 80s, and Carl Frank, in his 90s.

The old-timers who had come into the country at the turn of the century or shortly thereafter were dying or moving to one of the pioneer homes. Old-timers living in Wiseman in the 1940s included R.H. Creecy, Verne Watts, Charlie Irish, Hughie Boyle, Nick Ikovich, Wes Etherington, Ace Wilcox, and Mr. and Mrs. William English, Sr.

Bill English, Jr., and I became good friends

Members of the English family pose on the Wiseman airstrip in 1944. The photo shows, from left: Mrs. Mary English; Bill English, Jr.; Mary's daughter, Tishu Ulen; Tishu's son, Ben; and Bill English, Sr. (Walter Johnson)

Bill English, Jr. (left), and Walter Johnson stand next to Bill's Aeronica on the Wiseman airstrip in 1944. Bill and Walt became good friends in the early 1940s when both frequented the University of Alaska, Fairbanks — Walt attending classes and Bill attending the military training camp that had been set up on a part of the campus.
(Courtesy of Shirley English)

when he appeared on the University of Alaska campus at Fairbanks after being inducted into the service. The military had taken over a portion of the campus to use as a training camp. Bill was born in Coldfoot and spent his early years around Wiseman, but more recently had been attending school and living with relatives in California. On holidays and vacations we would visit his parents at Wiseman. When his father retired in 1944, after many years of managing the stores at Bettles and Wiseman, Bill and I purchased the Wiseman trading post. This included the store, warehouses, and living quarters. Mrs. Mary English, Bill's mother, continued to live in Wiseman. Mrs. English was also the mother of Tishu Ulen.

In mid-November 1945, Bill flew me to Wiseman for what was to be a two-week break from school at the university. He did not return to take me back to Fairbanks until the end of January, just in time to take my final examinations. Fortunately, I had

taken my books along. In any event, during those months I had plenty of time to cut a supply of wood for Mrs. English, to go caribou hunting with Arctic Johnnie, to help Hans Christensen with his mining near Big Lake, and to nearly memorize the several books I had with me.

After completing my first semester examinations, I returned to Wiseman in February with a modest shipment of supplies for the store, which had been closed for several years. That summer, and for the following six or seven years, I worked for the Alaska Road Commission, predecessor of the state Department of Transportation.

Each May it was a pleasure to return to Wiseman with a small stock of goods for the store and to resume work with the road commission. In late April or May ashes were scattered on the snow that covered the garden plots to hasten its melting. We always had greens from the garden to supplement canned and dried foods from the store.

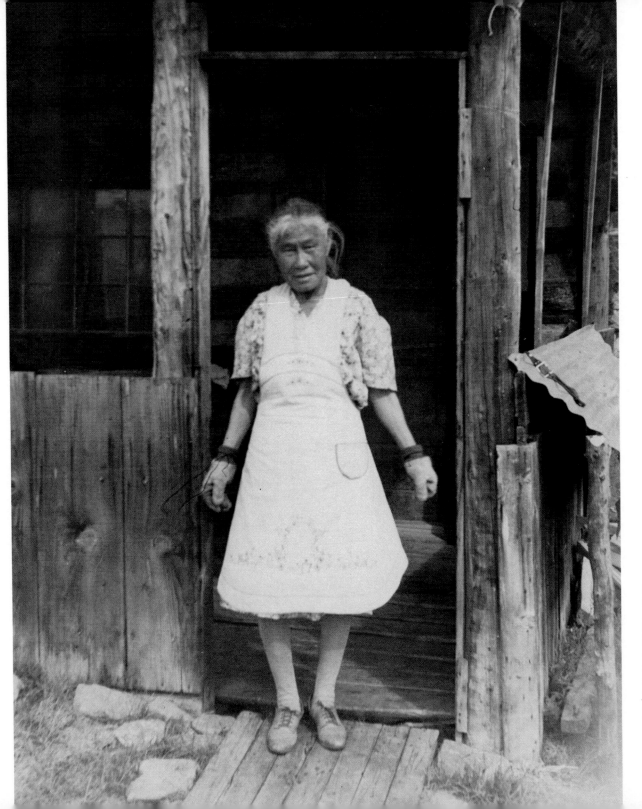

Mrs. Mary English stands in the doorway of her cabin in 1946. Mrs. English was known for the excellent bread she baked, and miners often came by her cabin for a loaf of fresh bread when they arrived in Wiseman from the creeks.
(Gordon Hilchey; courtesy of Walter Johnson)

This 1947 photo shows the trolley below Wiseman, part of the foot trail to Coldfoot. The Alaska Road Commission repaired or replaced the trolleys when they were damaged or destroyed by high water during spring breakup. (Walter Johnson)

Roads, Trails, and Airports

The old Alaska Road Commission was an essential part of small communities throughout Alaska for many decades, especially in those communities that had active mining. Each community would get a small appropriation to employ a few individuals for a few months.

Each spring we would go to the road commission office in Fairbanks and see Frank Nash, who was the supervisor for interior Alaska for many years. He would ask, "Are you going to Wiseman again?" Upon receiving a "Yes," he would say, "Well, what do you need?" A few barrels of fuel would be sent in for the old bulldozer and truck. He instructed us to write at least once a month and tell him what we were doing. In all the years I worked for the road commission at Wiseman, never once did a supervisor come to check our work. However, you can be sure that the local residents kept a close account of what we were doing. My fellow workers always laughed at the way I checked my watch frequently to be sure we worked our full eight hours each and every day.

The roads consisted of two seven-mile roads, one to Nolan Creek and one to Hammond River. There was also a 30-mile trail to Big Lake and a 17-mile trail to Coldfoot and Porcupine Creek. Trolleys suspended on a cable were provided across the Middle Fork of the Koyukuk a few miles above and below Wiseman for those who walked the trails. At first there were only two vehicles in Wiseman, Joe Ulen's pickup and the road commission dump truck. Later there were several jeeps.

(Right →) Syd Stealey stands in front of the cabin he stayed in while working for the Alaska Road Commission in Wiseman in 1947. The cabin is said to be the one Robert Marshall stayed in while he lived in Wiseman in 1929. Syd later became a dentist and now practices in Fairbanks. (Walter Johnson)

Walter Johnson washes clothes in front of the cabin in Wiseman in 1947. The truck on the right was used to haul water from the river, which was then heated in the barrel at left over an open fire.
(Courtesy of Walter Johnson)

Gathering Wood

Each fall, it seemed to be more difficult to get away from Wiseman. One of the problems was getting in enough wood to last Mrs. English for the winter. Throughout the years, trees suitable for firewood close to the town had been used. Some summers I would get up early in the morning and hike 10 or 12 miles above Wiseman, cut a cord of wood, tie it onto a raft, and float it down to town. On one such occasion, I arrived home tired close to midnight, tied up the raft, and went to bed. The sky was clear, but unfortunately, it had rained heavily at the head of the river. In the morning, to my dismay, the raft was gone. But all was not lost. Sammy Hope and his wife, Ludi, were then the only two residents living in Coldfoot. Sammy saw the raft coming downriver and with pleasure added it to his winter wood supply. Even in his 70s, Sammy would pole up the swift Middle Fork 11 miles from Coldfoot to Wiseman, working his longboat from shore to shore. On his next visit to Wiseman he reported with a chuckle finding the raft of wood.

It seemed that each fall it took me longer to complete my chores before returning to school. I've always been grateful to Ivar Skarland and Druska Carr (Schaible) for signing those slips that I could carry to Dean Duckering to regain my late entrance. The fall before graduation, when I meekly brought my class entrance slips from my ever-patient professors to the dean, he grabbed them and signed them, muttering, "What is the problem, Walter, you are only a month late this year? It seems that last year it was six weeks."

Wiseman in the 1940s

After World War II a few of the miners returned to the Koyukuk. However, the price of gold remained at $35 an ounce, hardly a strong incentive for mining.

Visitors to Wiseman were rather few, and still created somewhat of a stir on their arrival. One such visitor in 1946 was E.S. (Stu) Rabeau. He was on his first assignment as a young Public Health Service doctor at Kotzebue and had been brought to Wiseman in a small plane by Bill English. Except when Dr. Paul Haggland had come up from Fairbanks to visit his friend Bobby Jones, a doctor had not been in Wiseman for decades. Most of us were too taken by surprise, or too healthy, to marshal any complaints for his attention. Only George the Greek, with his unending lament about his arthritis, came forward as a likely patient. Dr. Rabeau was wearing his dark uniform with one and a half gold stripes, a source of amazement and amusement to all of us. Dr. Rabeau continued at Kotzebue for 15 years. Later in his career, he became director of the state Division of Public Health under Governor Hammond.

Occasionally on the Fourth of July, or when some family came back to Wiseman to visit, the population would swell to the point where we could open the Pioneer Hall and have a dance. There were old phonograph records in Wiseman, and I had brought a number of folk dance records from Fairbanks, where we had an active folk dance club. The old Pioneer Hall floor would shake again to the rhythms of polkas, schottisches, and waltzes. Eighty-five-year-old Hughie Boyle danced as nimbly as ever. Commissioner Charlie Irish danced with deliberation. When we tired of folk and round dances, Arctic Johnnie would bring out the drums and we would switch to Eskimo dancing.

Few young persons lived in Wiseman at that time: Florence Ulen, a few years younger than myself; her younger brother, Ben; and Lillian, adopted daughter of Arctic Johnnie and Esther. All of us left for school in the winter except Lillian, who went hunting with her parents, but did go off to school in Fairbanks later. Dorothy Jonas lived with her parents either in Wiseman or up at Big Lake.

Alcohol did not seem to be a great problem in the village. There was, of course, no liquor store. An

occasional bottle or two would arrive on the mail plane from Fairbanks, resulting in the conversation picking up in one of the cabins for an evening or two.

Old-Timers

Bobby Jones continued to live and mine on Nolan Creek. His partner, Kenneth Harvey, had gone to Fairbanks to work for Wien Airlines, now Wien Air Alaska. Smithy Wanamaker divided his time between Wiseman, Nolan, and going elsewhere for work. Verne Watts continued to live at Hammond River where he had been a very successful miner earlier, recovering one of the larger nuggets ever found in Alaska. He died in 1946 on Vermont Creek while showing the ground to George Miscovich. We brought him out in a sluice box tied to the blade of the old road commission Cat, which was the only piece of machinery available at the time that would make the trip beyond the end of the road. Wes Etherington built a coffin, I prepared the body, and Charlie Irish gave the memorial speech. He was then laid to rest among the birch trees on the hill above Wiseman. And so it was with one after another of the old-timers. Albert Ness, who lived in Knute Ellingson's old cabin near the store, had the misfortune of losing the cabin and huge book collection in a fire. Even though he was in his 80s, he built himself another cabin, which is still in use, at the other end of town. Albert Ness was an avid reader of history and foreign affairs throughout his long life. We

One of the old-timers in Wiseman in the 1940s was miner Nick Ikovich, shown in this 1937 photo standing by his cabin on Mascot Creek, about 12 miles west of town. Ikovich ran a groundsluicing operation on claims 6, 7, and 8 Above Discovery. (Reprinted from *Upper Koyukuk Region, Alaska,* Alaska Territorial Department of Mines, 1937)

(Above ↕) *Jack White, shown here in 1947, was a miner and freight hauler on the Koyukuk. Before the arrival of the Caterpiller in 1929, White used horses on the banks and bars of the river to pull barges of freight up the swift and shallow Koyukuk. Hay fields on the river flats near Wiseman provided feed for the horses in the winter.* (Walter Johnson)

(Right →) *Smithy Wanamaker, miner and longtime Wiseman resident, poses amid the blossoms in Ace Wilcox's potato patch in 1946. In his early days, Smithy would walk from Wiseman to Valdez, a distance of about 450 miles, when he wished to catch a ship to Seattle.* (Walter Johnson)

An unidentified young lady stands in Wiseman, with the old Plummer store in the background. The date of the photo is also unknown, but it was taken sometime prior to 1927, when the store burned.
(Courtesy of Wiseman Trading Company)

frequently exchanged periodicals, and I spent a great deal of time in his cabin having discussions. Among other things, he told me the history of every creek in the Koyukuk area, who had mined it, how much gold it had produced, and all of the details, most of which I have, to my regret, since forgotten.

Harry Leonard, currently the senior citizen of Wiseman, was mining on Gold Creek in the 1940s. He also kept a small stock of groceries which were for sale to the local people.

The Wiseman Store

As near as I can piece together, an individual by the name of Wright had a store at the mouth of Wiseman Creek at the time of the early stampede into the country. My guess is that the present store building was probably built around 1910. Some distance from the present store was another store building, somewhat larger. I believe this was operated first by Plummer and then by the Northern Commercial Company. The present store served as a warehouse. We have a picture of a young lady bedecked in furs standing in front of the Wiseman Trading Company living quarters with the larger store in the background. Her identity, unfortunately, has never been established. The larger store building burned to the ground in 1927, and the operation was moved to the present store building. In 1972, while in Wiseman, I removed the mercantile and tobacco licenses from the wall where they had been tacked. The first of these was issued to Sam Dubin in 1929, authorizing business under $50,000 per annum, and carrying a fee of $125. Subsequent licenses were tacked one upon the other to the log wall throughout the ensuing years. As an example, the license in 1940 was issued to the Wiseman Trading Company (English and Dubin) for the same amount and a similar fee. After the departure of the Northern Commercial Company, the store was operated for many years by Dubin and English, along with the stores at

Bettles and, in some years, Alatna, through the 1920s, 1930s, and mid-1940s. The records were meticulously kept by William D. English, Sr. The last license was issued in May 1946, authorizing under $4,000 in trade, and carrying a fee of $1.67, issued to the Wiseman Trading Company (English and Johnson) and signed by John B. Hall of Fairbanks.

Since almost everyone living in the Wiseman area during those years had some transaction with the store, their names are recorded in store records. In many cases the miners simply deposited their gold in Mr. English's care. He would weigh it on the old scales, send it off to the mint or bank, and credit the miner's account. From this, purchases were made, and other individuals' accounts were credited for wood, sewing, labor, and such activities. Consequently, these records provide an account of who lived in Wiseman and their activities through a number of decades. Many of the fixtures and other things from the store have disappeared over the years; however, there are still a few interesting items. One of these is a huge coffee grinder, probably brought in early in the century, about four feet in height, which stood on the store counter. There is an interesting collection of old medicines and surgical tools, some of which are probably 50 to 75 years old. As mentioned above, English and Johnson opened the store on a very modest scale in 1946. Mining did not return to the extent anticipated; the population of Wiseman remained small, and mining activities limited. Neither Mrs. English nor I were avid bookkeepers, and business was minimal. We resorted to the "open book" method. I simply listed the name of each individual or family that came to the store at the top of a page. When individuals took something from the store, they simply wrote it down on their page in the book, and when they came to pay, the account could be easily tallied up. Outsiders seldom came to Wiseman then, and if they did, they usually brought their own supplies.

Cora Dubin was the wife of Sam Dubin, entrepreneur of the Koyukuk from the 1920s to the 1940s. Mrs. Dubin operated businesses at Bettles and Wiseman in partnership with Bill English, Sr. The first Caterpiller was brought to the Koyukuk in 1929 by English and Dubin to haul freight between Bettles and Wiseman. (Courtesy of Wiseman Trading Company)

In November 1948, when I left Wiseman to go Outside to apply for medical school, few articles were left in the store. Those items not damaged by freezing were moved into the warehouse, and those that could be damaged were stacked on shelves in the cabin. As Mrs. English used or sold these items, the Wiseman store quietly slipped, after 50 years, into the past as a business. However, the building itself continued to stand. I had repaired the iron sheet roof the best I could. One of the warehouses

was torn down and used for firewood. Another was sold and moved to Nolan Creek. In the mid-1950s and several times during the 1960s, I returned to Wiseman to check on the buildings and to cut back the brush and grass. In 1970 the store and house were leased to Glen Bouton and Ernie Gilbert, who did some work on the buildings. Pete Pasquali, who lived in the house one winter, repaired the roof and made other improvements. Later, Vern Bouton, son of Glen Bouton, lived in the house while working for the Department of Transportation out of the Coldfoot camp. Currently the old store building is leased to Dan Wetzel, who is repairing the foundation. Mr. Wetzel uses the building as headquarters for his hunting and bird-watching expeditions. I hope that with a tight roof and a shored-up foundation, this old log building can stand another 75 years in the arctic climate.

Most of both the year-round and summer residents of Wiseman seem to prefer that the village remain quiet, free of commerce, and that traffic in and out be kept to a minimum. Coldfoot, only 11 miles away, now offers fuel, grocery supplies, and has a restaurant, mainly to serve the truckers on the haul road. The road into Wiseman from the haul road is all but impassable except with four-wheel drive.

Trees and Plants

Ace Wilcox, early market hunter and gardener at Wiseman, reports that early in the century the surrounding country was covered with spruce and birch, with many less willows and alders than exist

Ace Wilcox stands in one of his potato patches in the summer of 1946. Ace was an early meat hunter, often traveling great distances to obtain game. During the summer months, the meat was stored in an ice cave dug into the permafrost in the riverbank across from the village. (Walter Johnson)

A four-wheel-drive vehicle fords Wiseman Creek, the only way to get from the north to the south side of town. In 1959, Jim Johnson and others converted the vehicle bridge across the creek to a foot bridge.
(Walter Johnson)

today. Within Wiseman itself, the spruce were chopped down and the grass and brush were kept cut with a scythe so that the entire town was treeless, as it appears in early photographs. As the population dwindled in the 1930s and 1940s, willows and balsam cottonwood sprang up. Even a few young spruce began to return. By the 1950s, some of the cabins were almost overgrown. Construction of the pipeline and haul road generated sporadic interest in Wiseman with some of the cabins being purchased and rebuilt. Today the brush has been cut back, although a number of the trees have been spared. Spruce trees are returning. Some of the old footpaths are overgrown, but now

there is evidence of vehicle traffic on the road through town.

For decades there were only two vehicles, then Harry Leonard's jeep and others, but now traffic within the village, while not heavy, is common. The bridge across Wiseman Creek at one time carried light vehicles. However, a number of years ago it was replaced with a foot bridge so that now vehicles cross from one side of Wiseman to the other by driving through the stream at its mouth.

Tony Tomisch made the interesting observation that North Wiseman, that is, north of the stream, tends to be a mining community, and South Wiseman the place for gardeners.

Population and People

Of the handful of more permanent residents, there are three who arrived before 1950. Harry Leonard came into the country in 1934 and has been there continuously ever since. At 85, he is Wiseman's oldest resident. Charles Breck, the current unofficial mayor and postmaster of Wiseman, by my recollection began coming to Wiseman from the North Fork of the Koyukuk in 1947 and 1948. He later purchased the Ace Wilcox estate, reduced the cabin and gardens to a more manageable size, and has lived there since. Ross Brockman came into the country in the late 1940s, first settling upriver and later moving into Wiseman, where he has been an avid gardener and gatherer of local plants. The number of cabins in Wiseman has been much reduced by removal for firewood. Those remaining are for the most part being kept in a fair state of repair, with the exception of the roadhouse, which with its sod roof has fallen down in recent years.

Pipeline Impact

When the pipeline and haul road were approved, there was a renewed interest in the Koyukuk. Souvenir seekers thoughtlessly came through and picked up what artifacts they could find around the old cabins. Currently, the Bureau of Land Management and local residents do a rather good job of preventing this sort of activity.

The haul road has made a big difference. Now local residents can drive to Fairbanks for supplies.

Flattened oil drums make up the roof of the Wiseman cabin formerly occupied by Ace Wilcox. Although fireweed has taken over Ace's huge potato patch, the cabin is still in good condition, and is now occupied by Charlie Breck, unofficial mayor of Wiseman. (Walter Johnson)

Mount Sukakpak (4,200 feet) sweeps skyward near the junction of the Middle Fork Koyukuk, Dietrich, and Bettles rivers. The trans-Alaska pipeline runs through the valley of the Middle Fork. (Gil Mull)

However, the route is not an easy drive, with steep grades and heavy truck traffic. The quietness that formerly characterized Wiseman is now broken by the hundred or more trucks that may pass in a day on the haul road just across the river from town. Even more remarkable is the cloud of dust that hangs over the entire valley during dry periods in the summer. The mail plane comes twice a month from Bettles, and small planes land occasionally.

Now and Then

Wiseman is proof that no place in the world is far away any more. Remoteness is probably a word that we can soon drop from the language, as the globe and Alaska continue to fill up with people. The Brooks Range, while pleasant, is not necessarily an easy place to make a living. Game is not all that abundant, except in the rare times when the caribou come by, and certainly cannot sustain heavy pressure from hunting. However, the land does hold a certain attraction for some people. When I was 20 I promised myself that I would return to the upper Koyukuk and again hike the surrounding mountains. In 1972, when I was 50, my two young sons and I did just that and had a very pleasant trip. In fact, it was so much fun that, with my son Charlie and friend Anne, I did the same in the summer of 1982. A year ago Tishu Ulen and family were vacationing in Wiseman at the same time my son and I were visiting. It was strange to be living in our same cabins a few feet apart, as we had 35 years earlier. Tishu's ever-present sense of humor and ready laugh had not changed. She has had a full rich life in the Koyukuk, and it was easy to see how happy she was to be back.

Although Wiseman has changed with the coming of the pipeline, it still has a certain charm and timelessness. It seems to be a village that refuses to grow and refuses to die, a certain defiance of the rules of nature and economics.

This is not a history of Wiseman, but simply one individual's impressions. And although the number of people in Wiseman at any one time is few, I'm sure that this village has touched the lives of many. A few years ago I made the remark to Ross Brockman, one of the long-term residents, "Wiseman is changing; it seems to be picking up." Ross's comment was, "Yeah, we used to have nothing, and now we don't even have that."

Harry Leonard (left) and Walter Johnson stop to reminisce in front of the old Wiseman Trading Company. Harry came to the Koyukuk in 1934 and mined on Gold and Nolan creeks. At 85, he is presently the oldest resident of Wiseman. (Anne Wieland)

Fish Camp: Koyukuk Style

Story and photos by Joseph Agnese

Editor's note: *Joseph Agnese was a faculty member and graduate student in the geography department of Portland (Oregon) State University prior to spending six months in 1982 in Alaska's Interior working for the Bureau of Indian Affairs. He is anxious to return and make Alaska his home.*

I had always dreamed of visiting Alaska. That dream came true when the Bureau of Indian Affairs accepted me for temporary duty, identifying and evaluating cemetery sites and historic places claimed by Native corporations under the Alaska Native Claims Settlement Act. Alaska Natives would assist me in my field work.

One of our field camps was on the Indian River, near the abandoned mining camp of Utopia. From there, we had to travel twice weekly to the Athabascan village of Hughes, where we picked up and delivered mail for our crew. Hughes is a sleepy village nestled below a bluff overlooking the Koyukuk River, less than 35 miles from the Arctic Circle. The village consists of about 40 cabins, a general store, a school, and an airstrip. A cabin doubles as the post office. In this cabin we met many of the villagers as we awaited the arrival of the mail plane.

One day, while sitting in the mail cabin, I struck up a conversation with Bill Williams. As we talked, it turned out that I had been guided to several historic sites by his father, Levine. I told Bill how much I enjoyed the helicopter trips with his dad, and the spark of friendship was ignited.

The next week I saw Bill again. The chum salmon were beginning their annual run, and Bill had a rack of fish drying along the bank of the river. As I admired his catch, Bill told me that he was anxious to go to his summer fish camp, 24 miles downstream. He told me he had already taken his wife, Madeline, and their children to the camp, and that Levine and his wife had taken their boat and joined the family there too.

"I sure wish I was going along with you," I said. "I know that it must be a really wonderful experience."

Bill smiled and said, "It's quite a bit of work, too. Why don't you come along and see?"

Wishing I could accept the invitation, I

Neat log cabins stand in rows in the tiny Native village of Hughes, on the east bank of the lower Koyukuk River. The 1980 census reported 71 residents of Hughes.

Bureau of Indian Affairs workers arrange tents over tent frames while setting up their camp on the Indian River near the deserted gold camp of Utopia.

couldn't help thinking about our work schedule of 10 hours a day, six days a week. This didn't leave much time for personal pursuits.

Returning to camp, I mentioned the invitation to Jim, my tent-mate and co-worker, and an avid amateur photographer. He was really enthused.

"If you can get that invitation extended to include me also, I'll wager that I can talk the boss into giving us some time off for a mid-season break," Jim proposed.

I agreed to the plan, and by the following weekend Bill had extended his invitation to include both of us, and our leave had been granted.

It was mid-July and the peak of the salmon run as Jim and I piled out of the helicopter at Hughes with all the gear we would need for our stay at fish camp. Bill met us at the airstrip and helped us load our gear into the 14-foot, handmade boat that was powered with a 20-hp motor. We made quick arrangements with our pilot to be picked up later and were headed downstream almost before the helicopter had left its pad.

We had seen the river countless times from the air and thought we knew it well. From above there didn't seem to be a single straight stretch of water, but it was different traveling on it. The river seemed huge and straight. The only clue to direction change was the different position of the sun on the horizon. We saw black bear along each side of the river, and Bill pointed out the sand bar that had provided last year's moose. After about an hour on the river, we nosed the boat into fish camp.

Clambering up the bank with our gear, we stacked our supplies in the cook tent and said hello to Madeline. She handed us steaming mugs of hot coffee. There was little small talk, but we were made to feel at home and had a chance to explore the camp. It was located on the riverbank and consisted of three canvas cabin tents on wooden frames arranged in a circle around a central structure. This structure was used for cooking and eating and provided a covered area to protect drying fish from wet weather. Several cache pits, dug down to the permafrost, provided natural refrigeration. Three fish racks, partially filled with salmon, and a large area where several dozen dogs were staked completed the camp.

After bidding our hosts good night, we picked a convenient cleared spot near a neatly stacked pile of firewood and pitched our bright orange tent. The dogs soon settled down as they accepted our presence in camp and, exhausted but exhilarated, we soon drifted off to sleep.

We awakened to the sound of salmon thrashing and jumping in the pool beside our tent and the smell of bacon and coffee. We scrambled to the cook tent, not wanting to look too eager, and watched the mist rising from the river as Madeline prepared a breakfast of pancakes, eggs, and bacon. Soon the children appeared from their tent, tentatively approaching as they became aware of two strangers in their midst. We offered them cookies and juice from our supplies, and soon they were smiling. Our first day in fish camp was beginning.

Bill Williams (left) engages in a relaxed conversation with the author.

Fishnets were in place and producing well. For the last week they had been netting about 100 fish a day. Bill had discovered the best places for the nets after years of trial and error.

"The nets have to be kept in eddies," Bill explained, "or the current will just fill them with junk. Then the fish can see the nets, and we won't catch them. Want to come out and see the nets?"

"Sure," I replied, "just try to treat us like family. We want to try to be a part of camp and help out as much as possible."

We climbed into the boat and sped downstream to check the nets. It is amazing how tangled a

Bill and Madeline Williams's fish camp stands on the bank above the Koyukuk River, 24 miles downstream from Hughes.

salmon can get in a net. Most were enmeshed to their gills and were small enough to pull through. But some of the bigger fish were caught by their hooked snouts and jutting toothed jaws. It took the novices in the group quite a while to untangle them. Bill and Madeline waited patiently for Jim and me to finish a job they could have finished with ease.

After checking all three of the nets, we had three containers, 55-gallon drums that had been cut in half, filled with more than 50 fish. Most of the fish were chum salmon, but there were five king salmon and two whitefish. Madeline was especially happy to see the whitefish, which she considered a special delicacy.

As Jim and I unloaded the boat, Bill, Madeline, and their oldest son, Victor, set up fish cutting tables at the edge of the river. The tables were big enough to accommodate a large salmon, and each had a nail, point end up, embedded in its lower right corner.

Bill and Victor started with the chum salmon. After cutting off the toothy snout, the anal and dorsal fins were removed. The salmon was then impaled, through the fleshy part above the base of the tail, on the nail in the table. A sharp, pointed filleting knife was inserted into the back of the fish at the tail, just above the backbone. A quick forward thrust of the knife, cutting close to and following the backbone, exited through the nose and separated the top fillet. This part was allowed to hang over the right side of the table. Another cut was made in the same manner, except this time the backbone was severed near the tail, and the forward thrust cut close to and under the backbone. This separated the backbone from the fish and exposed the viscera. A quick scrape of the knife severed the gills, which were disposed of with the viscera. The process was completed with lateral cuts at about one-inch intervals through the fillets to the skins. These cuts exposed more flesh to the air and facilitated drying. All that remained were

Although the primary catch is chum salmon, Bill's fishnets yield an occasional surprise, such as this huge king which weighed more than 50 pounds.

the two fillets connected by their skin to the tail, which could be easily hung over a pole to dry in smoke for eventual use as dog food. Small smoky fires were always kept lit under the drying racks, and the direction of the breeze kept the smoke constantly filtering over the drying fish, causing the flesh to glaze over quickly.

Madeline cut all the king salmon, using a different technique. Instead of a filleting knife, she used a *tlaabaas*, a curved-bladed knife much like the Eskimo *ulu*. Instead of cutting close to the

(Left ←) *Using a curved-bladed knife called a* tlaabaas, *Madeline deftly cuts king salmon fillets into long thin strips. The fish will then be smoked and dried.*

(Below ↓) *Bill holds up a chum salmon, ready for the rack, showing the lateral cuts which facilitate the drying process.*

Chum salmon hang over the drying rack at the fish camp, ensuring a good supply of dog food for the winter.

(Above ↕) *Madeline Williams expertly applies beadwork to a moosehide slipper.*

(Right →) *This aerial of the lower Koyukuk, taken from a helicopter, shows the twisting course the river takes as it meanders through the lowlands of Alaska's Interior.*

backbone, she divided the fillet equally, leaving half of it connected to the backbone and half connected to the skin. She cut the meat on the backbone and hung that portion to dry in much the same manner as chum salmon. The part of the fillet nearest the skin, without any bones, was cut lengthwise into long, narrow strips to be dried specifically for human consumption.

Bill explained that the dogs, which were kept staked all summer, were important as transportation during the trapping season. Some Natives from the village prefer snow machines, but Bill feels that the machine's convenience is outweighed by the dog team's reliability, an important factor when trapping alone.

"One bum spark plug and you might freeze," Bill told me. "But if one dog dies, I can still make it back home."

Dogs require a lot of food, and these well-spawned chum salmon provide the bulk of their feed. While there are occasional jobs in construction in Hughes and other accessible locations, Bill relies upon himself and the land to provide for his family. He hunts moose for meat, his fish camp supplies food for his family and his dogs, and his trapline provides raw materials for Madeline's sewing and some much needed extra cash.

The trip to tend nets was repeated that evening. Jim and I managed to improve our removal techniques a bit. After we returned and prepared another boatload of salmon to dry on the rack, Madeline called us to the cook tent for a meal of moose stew, fish-head soup, smoked salmon, freshly baked bread, and hot coffee.

After dinner, Madeline brought out her sewing and started working on an exquisite pair of slippers. She had cut the pattern from moose hide and trimmed the slippers with beaver fur, both provided by Bill. Now she was adding beadwork.

The next few days we spent tending nets and cutting fish. Madeline instructed us in fish cutting. We worked hard, helping with other chores in the camp. We had a sense of satisfaction now, knowing we could really be of some help to these people who had shared a little bit of their lives with us.

Our last night in camp, we sat around the fire and discussed changes that had come to the Koyukon people. Bill remembered winter as a child as being a time of trapping and visiting, a time for family to be together. But now when the children get older, they must leave the village to go to school. Bill had children attending school in both Tanana and Fairbanks. Now he says that summer is the time to be together. The fish camp serves that purpose. Bill seldom sees his boys during trapping season and feels that they may be being deprived of an old and worthwhile skill. We also talked about his concern for the future of subsistence hunting. He told me stories of "slob" hunters who land on river bars, kill a moose, and fly away with the antlers, leaving the carcass to rot.

"The country is our life, and gives us our living. If people outside are allowed to kill game that we use for food, how will we eat?" he questioned.

Bill does not want his children to live like him. He wants a better life for them.

"But where will they work, and how will they feed themselves?"

We both knew there was no easy answer to that question.

"See you at five in the morning," Bill said, and after a long look around, we retired for the last time at the fish camp.

The sounds of the coffee pot were enough to jolt us awake at five. We broke down the tent and grabbed a quick cup of coffee. Then we loaded the boat again for the trip upriver to Hughes.

Back at the village, we relaxed as we awaited the helicopter that would return us to our Indian River camp. We reflected on the past few days and knew that we had had much more than a short vacation. We had a brief interlude into a different special kind of life, one that had its roots deep in the past. We were sure we would never forget this trip.

The Koyukuk Today

Life along the Koyukuk today remains much as it has been in the past. Most of the people live by subsistence or a combination of subsistence and cash income. Some earn a living by guiding, some by mining, and a few by working for the government.

Fish are the lifeblood of those living by subsistence. Many of the Koyukuk River's tributaries are spawning streams for salmon. The river itself is closed to commercial fishermen, but three residents of the village of Koyukuk (population 95) operate fish wheels on the Yukon River. They sell their catch to the commercial fish buyer at Galena, 28 miles upstream from the mouth of the Koyukuk.

For the last five years, subsistence fishermen have taken between 300 and 700 king salmon per year from the Koyukuk. Their catch of chum and coho salmon ranged between 15,000 and 30,000 in 1981. Much of this fish is dried for dog food. After the summer salmon runs, villagers net whitefish later in the fall.

Hunters seek moose, caribou, black bear, and smaller mammals to replenish their meat supplies. In winter, trappers search out beaver, fox, lynx, marten, mink, and wolf.

Doyon Limited represents most of the region's Natives from its headquarters in Fairbanks. The village corporations of Huslia, Hughes, Allakaket, and Alatna have banded together under K'oyitł ots'ina, Limited to deal

Living by subsistence in Koyukuk country means taking advantage of the area's wildlife resources. Residents catch fish in summer and fall; hunt in spring, summer, and fall; and trap in winter. One of the larger game animals is the moose whose carcass provides plenty of fresh meat and whose hide, such as this one hanging to dry at Allakaket, is tanned and made into clothing and other household items. (USFWS)

with local problems. Claude Demientieff, Jr., general manager of the combined village corporations, says that their goals for the next couple of years are to secure the villagers' land and finances. The combined corporations "want to be firmly situated in the business community," says Demientieff. K'oyitł ots'ina operates stores and lodges in Hughes (population 71) and Huslia (population 230) and has an interest in a construction company. Demientieff explains that they would like to move into regional business and real estate.

Bringing supplies into Koyukuk country is costly. Many bulk items come by barges pushed by tugboats, the powerful work horses of Alaska's interior rivers. Claude Demientieff, Sr., of Holy Cross, operates the tugboat *Ramona* on the Yukon, Tanana, and Koyukuk rivers. The *Rampart*, one of a fleet of tugboats under the flag of Yutana Barge Lines from Nenana, pushes barges up the Koyukuk as far as Hughes.

At Bettles (population 94) and farther up the Koyukuk, subsistence gives way to some extent. As a major access point for Gates of the Arctic National Park and Preserve, Bettles earns some income from outdoor enthusiasts anxious to explore the Brooks Range. Guides and river-running outfitters operate out of Bettles. The Federal Aviation Administration maintains a flight service station here.

Evansville, and adjacent Bettles Field, spread out along a bend of the Koyukuk River. The original town of Bettles was founded five miles downstream on a narrow creek next to the river. However, that site lacked a suitable area for building an airstrip; thus, in the 1940s a landing strip was built upstream. That strip was named Bettles Field, and the town that grew up around it was called Evansville (1980 population was 94). For many years, however, the entire community has been called Bettles, and the original townsite downriver has been referred to as Old Bettles. (Kit Marrs)

At the turn of the century miners roamed the Koyukuk. Today, gold-bearing quartz veins, and their associated placer deposits, still attract fortune seekers. The area has produced a little more than 500,000 ounces of gold with more than 51,000 ounces of silver as a by-product, most the result of placer mining from two regions: around Wiseman; and near Hughes, about 60 miles downstream from Allakaket on the lower Koyukuk.

The initial rush to the area around Wiseman began around the turn of the century and ended by 1920. Intermittent mining continued there through the early 1960s, with prospectors concentrating on streams already proven to contain gold. A period of dormancy followed, mainly because of high operating costs and the fixed $35 per ounce price of gold.

In recent years, rising gold prices and construction of the Dalton Highway, a service road which follows the trans-Alaska pipeline from Livengood in Alaska's Interior to Prudhoe Bay, have revived interest in gold mining. The highway provides

K'oyitł ots'ina, the combined village corporation for Huslia, Hughes, Alatna, and Allakaket, is supporting commerce and construction among these villages along the lower Koyukuk. These workers at Huslia are putting up a new cold storage building which will be thickly insulated and require no special coolants. Next door is the new community hall.
(Penny Rennick, staff)

137

The sister communities of Allakaket (below) and Alatna lie on opposite sides of the Koyukuk at its confluence with the Alatna River. Allakaket (population 158) is an Athabascan community; smaller Alatna (population about 30) is predominately Eskimo.
(George Wuerthner, below; Joseph Agnese, right)

These rafters paddle the Alatna River, a major tributary of the Koyukuk. Several guides and river-running outfitters operate from Bettles, a central location for exploring the Gates of the Arctic, and the Kobuk and Noatak rivers to the west.
(John and Margaret Ibbotson)

access to many of the creeks whose wealth brought them fame during the gold rush — Slate, Nolan, Minnie, Marion, and Gold creeks, the Hammond River, and upper portions of the South and Middle forks of the Koyukuk itself. In 1981 the state Division of Geological and Geophysical Surveys reported that mechanized equipment, small suction dredges, and one drift mine were working on at least a dozen upper Koyukuk streams.

Although gold brought the upper Koyukuk into the limelight, the area holds a wealth of other minerals. Recent reports by the U.S. Geological Survey indicate high concentrations of uranium in stream sediments around Mount Doonerak. The reports also show geologic anomalies in the upper Koyukuk drainage similar to those of the Ambler mineral belt to the west, and some speculate that the Koyukuk may hold similar mineral potential.

Other exploration has uncovered varying quantities of silver, copper, mercury, antimony, molybdenum, lead, and arsenic. The only significant production, however, came during World War II, when Alamco, Inc., recovered five tons of the strategic mineral stibnite (antimony sulfide) from Smith Creek, the major gold-producing tributary of Nolan Creek.

In 1938 coal was reported in the bedrock of Mailbox Creek, a tributary of the Middle Fork Koyukuk, southwest of Wiseman. Commercial exploitation of this coal was never accomplished, but early miners at Tramway Bar used it to fuel their boilers. More recently, a bed of bituminous coal has been discovered about 36 miles northeast of Bettles along the Middle Fork.

During construction of the pipeline and haul road, several pits were opened along the upper reaches of the South and Middle forks to provide both crushed stone and sand and gravel for construction.

On the lower Koyukuk River, present mining activity is limited. Gold was first discovered in this area around the turn of the century, but only

Panning is one method of extracting gold from the rich earth of the Koyukuk. Normally, however, miners rely on sluice boxes, and in the case of large deposits, on floating dredges.
(Steve McCutcheon)

(Above ↟) *This aerial shows the Alaska Gold Company dredge at Hogatza, 37 miles west of Hughes. U. S. Smelting, Refining, and Mining Company operated the dredge from 1957 to 1975, when it was shut down. Operations were resumed by Alaska Gold in 1981, and dredging continued throughout the 1982 season.* (Joseph Agnese)

(Right→) *A large bucket line dredge, now operated by Alaska Gold Company, works Bear Creek at Hogatza in 1975. Buckets at the front of the dredge scoop up the earth, which is then carried inside by conveyor belt to where the gold is separated from the waste material. This waste is then passed out the back of the dredge, leaving behind neat rows of gravel tailings.* (Gilbert R. Eakins, DGGS)

scattered, intermittent development took place until 1938, when a non-float, dragline-fed placer mine began operation on Utopia Creek. Incomplete records indicate activities on this creek ceased in 1962.

United States Smelting, Refining, and Mining Company began exploring on Bear Creek near Hogatza, about 42 miles northwest of Hughes, in 1939. Eventually a dredge originally installed at Livengood was transported to Hogatza and began operating in 1957. The dredge was shut down in 1975 but reactivated in 1981 by Alaska Gold Company, which operates dredges at Nome. The dredge on Bear Creek mined through the 1982 field season.

Thus the rich earth still lures fortune seekers to this remote region; the land still provides for the area's few permanent residents; and the Koyukuk River, main artery for about 30,000 square miles of northcentral Alaska, still flows.

Guide Bernd Gaedeke (standing left) runs Iniakuk Lake Lodge in the Brooks Range northwest of Bettles. Gaedeke and John Ibbotson watch as Rachael (with pan) and Johnny Gaedeke help scoop up water from the lake. (John and Margaret Ibbotson)

Autumn colors glow under the fleeting sunshine of a cloud-filled sky in this shot of the North Fork Koyukuk Valley near Long Lake and Delay Pass, due west of Wiseman. (Jon Nickles)

(Above ↑) *Bill Fickus and his son, Matt, make repairs at their ranch on Crevice Creek in the valley of the John River which flows into the Koyukuk near Bettles.* (Bill Sherwonit)

(Right →) *The fishing is good in Koyukuk country. Here Tim Fickus strains to lift a 10-pound northern pike.* (Bill Sherwonit)

Fishermen motor along the Koyukuk, 15 miles upriver from its junction with the Yukon. (USFWS)

Ray Bane and his wife, Barbara, make their home in Bettles where Ray works as a subsistence field coordinator for the National Park Service. A teacher, pilot, trapper, and all-around bush resident, Ray has lived along the Koyukuk, first at Hughes and now Bettles, for many years studying the culture, traditional trading routes, and methods of communication among the Koyukon people.
(George Wuerthner)

(Above ↑) *Campers find what shelter they can among the low vegetation in the Valley of Precipices. The view south shows the twin peaks that have become the Gates of the Arctic, Boreal Mountain (left) and Frigid Crags.* (Jon Nickles)

(Right →) *Pillars of the Gates of the Arctic, 6,666-foot Boreal Mountain (shown here) and its neighbor to the west, Frigid Crags (5,550 feet) flank the North Fork Koyukuk and were designated Gates of the Arctic by Robert Marshall in the 1920s.* (Jon Nickles)

Alaska Geographic® Back Issues

The North Slope, Vol. 1, No. 1. The charter issue of *ALASKA GEOGRAPHIC*® took a long, hard look at the North Slope and the then-new petroleum development at "the top of the world." *Out of print.*

One Man's Wilderness, Vol. 1, No. 2. The story of a dream shared by many, fulfilled by few: a man goes into the bush, builds a cabin and shares his incredible wilderness experience. Color photos. 116 pages, $9.95

Admiralty . . . Island in Contention, Vol. 1, No. 3. An intimate and multifaceted view of Admiralty: its geological and historical past, its present-day geography, wildlife and sparse human population. Color photos. 78 pages, $5.00

Fisheries of the North Pacific: History, Species, Gear & Processes, Vol. 1, No. 4. The title says it all. This volume is out of print, but the book, from which it was excerpted, is available in a revised, expanded large-format volume. 424 pages. $24.95.

The Alaska-Yukon Wild Flowers Guide, Vol. 2, No. 1. First Northland flower book with both large, color photos and detailed drawings of every species described. Features 160 species, common and scientific names and growing height. Vertical-format book edition now available. 218 pages, $12.95.

Richard Harrington's Yukon, Vol. 2, No. 2. The Canadian province with the colorful past *and* present. *Out of print.*

Prince William Sound, Vol. 2, No. 3. This volume explored the people and resources of the Sound. *Out of print.*

Yakutat: The Turbulent Crescent, Vol. 2, No. 4. History, geography, people — and the impact of the coming of the oil industry. *Out of print.*

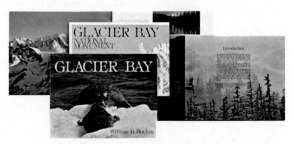

Glacier Bay: Old Ice, New Land, Vol. 3, No. 1. The expansive wilderness of Southeastern Alaska's Glacier Bay National Monument (recently proclaimed a national park and preserve) unfolds in crisp text and color photographs. Records the flora and fauna of the area, its natural history, with hike and cruise information, plus a large-scale color map. 132 pages, $11.95

The Land: Eye of the Storm, Vol. 3, No. 2. The future of one of the earth's biggest pieces of real estate! *This volume is out of print,* but the latest on the Alaska lands controversy is detailed completely in Volume 8, Number 4.

Alaska's Volcanoes: Northern Link in the Ring of Fire, Vol. 4, No. 1. Scientific overview supplemented with eyewitness accounts of Alaska's historic volcano eruptions. Includes color and black-and-white photos and a schematic description of the effects of plate movement upon volcanic activity. 88 pages. *Temporarily out of print.*

Wilderness Proposals: Which Way for Alaska's Lands?, Vol. 4, No. 4. This volume gave yet another detailed analysis of the many Alaska lands questions. *Out of print.*

Richard Harrington's Antarctic, Vol. 3, No. 3. The Canadian photojournalist guides readers through remote and little understood regions of the Antarctic and Subantarctic. More than 200 color photos and a large fold-out map. 104 pages, $8.95

The Brooks Range: Environmental Watershed, Vol. 4, No. 2. An impressive work on a truly impressive piece of Alaska — The Brooks Range. *Out of print.*

Cook Inlet Country, Vol. 5, No. 1. Our first comprehensive look at the area. A visual tour of the region — its communities, big and small, and its countryside. Begins at the southern tip of the Kenai Peninsula, circles Turnagain Arm and Knik Arm for a close-up view of Anchorage, and visits the Matanuska and Susitna valleys and the wild, west side of the inlet. *Out of print.*

The Silver Years of the Alaska Canned Salmon Industry: An Album of Historical Photos, Vol. 3, No. 4. The grand and glorious past of the Alaska canned salmon industry. *Out of print.*

Kodiak: Island of Change, Vol. 4, No. 3. Russians, wildlife, logging and even petroleum . . . an island where change is one of the few constants. *Out of print.*

Southeast: Alaska's Panhandle, Vol. 5, No. 2. Explores Southeastern Alaska's maze of fjords and islands, mossy forests and glacier-draped mountains — from Dixon Entrance to Icy Bay, including all of the state's fabled Inside Passage. Along the way are profiles of every town, together with a look at the region's history, economy, people, attractions and future. Includes large fold-out map and seven area maps. 192 pages, $12.95.

Bristol Bay Basin, Vol. 5, No. 3. Explores the land and the people of the region known to many as the commercial salmon-fishing capital of Alaska. Illustrated with contemporary color and historic black-and-white photos. Includes a large fold-out map of the region. *Out of print.*

The Aurora Borealis, Vol. 6, No. 2. Here one of the world's leading experts — Dr. S.-I. Akasofu of the University of Alaska — explains in an easily understood manner, aided by many diagrams and spectacular color and black-and-white photos, what causes the aurora, how it works, how and why scientists are studying it today and its implications for our future. 96 pages, $7.95.

Alaska's Great Interior, Vol. 7, No. 1. Alaska's rich Interior country, west from the Alaska-Yukon Territory border and including the huge drainage between the Alaska Range and the Brooks Range, is covered thoroughly. Included are the region's people, communities, history, economy, wilderness areas and wildlife. Illustrated with contemporary color and black-and-white photos. Includes a large fold-out map. 128 pages, $9.95.

Alaska Whales and Whaling, Vol. 5, No. 4. The wonders of whales in Alaska — their life cycles, travels and travails — are examined, with an authoritative history of commercial and subsistence whaling in the North. Includes a fold-out poster of 14 major whale species in Alaska in perspective, color photos and illustrations, with historical photos and line drawings. 144 pages, $12.95.

Alaska's Native People, Vol. 6, No. 3. In this edition the editors examine the varied worlds of the Inupiat Eskimo, Yup'ik Eskimo, Athabascan, Aleut, Tlingit, Haida and Tsimshian. Included are sensitive, informative articles by Native writers, plus a large, four-color map detailing the Native villages and defining the language areas. 304 pages, $24.95.

A Photographic Geography of Alaska, Vol. 7, No. 2. An overview of the entire state — a visual tour through the six regions of Alaska: Southeast, Southcentral/Gulf Coast, Alaska Peninsula and Aleutians, Bering Sea Coast, Arctic and Interior. Plus a handy appendix of valuable information — ''Facts About Alaska.'' Approximately 160 color and black-and-white photos and 35 maps. 192 pages. Revised in 1983. $15.95.

Yukon-Kuskokwim Delta, Vol. 6, No. 1. This volume explored the people and lifestyles of one of the most remote areas of the 49th state. *Out of print.*

The Stikine, Vol. 6, No 4. River route to three Canadian gold strikes in the 1800s. This edition explores 400 miles of Stikine wilderness, recounts the river's paddlewheel past and looks into the future. Illustrated with contemporary color photos and historic black-and-white; includes a large fold-out map. 96 pages, $9.95.

The Aleutians, Vol. 7, No. 3. Home of the Aleut, a tremendous wildlife spectacle, a major World War II battleground and now the heart of a thriving new commercial fishing industry. Contemporary color and black-and-white photographs, and a large fold-out map. 224 pages, $14.95.

Alaska Mammals, Vol. 8, No. 2. From tiny ground squirrels to the powerful polar bear, and from the tundra hare to the magnificent whales inhabiting Alaska's waters, this volume includes 80 species of mammals found in Alaska. Included are beautiful color photographs and personal accounts of wildlife encounters. 184 pages, $12.95.

Alaska's Glaciers, Vol. 9, No. 1. Examines in-depth the massive rivers of ice, their composition, exploration, present-day distribution and scientific significance. Illustrated with many contemporary color and historical black-and-white photos, the text includes separate discussions of more than a dozen glacial regions. 144 pages, $9.95.

Klondike Lost: A Decade of Photographs by Kinsey & Kinsey, Vol. 7, No. 4. An album of rare photographs and all-new text about the lost Klondike boom town of Grand Forks, second in size only to Dawson during the gold rush. Introduction by noted historian Pierre Berton: 138 pages, area maps and more than 100 historical photos, most never before published. $12.95.

The Kotzebue Basin, Vol. 8, No. 3. Examines northwestern Alaska's thriving trading area of Kotzebue Sound and the Kobuk and Noatak river basins. Contemporary color and historical black-and-white photographs. 184 pages, $12.95.

Sitka and Its Ocean/Island World, Vol. 9, No. 2. From the elegant capital of Russian America to a beautiful but modern port, Sitka, on Baranof Island, has become a commercial and cultural center for Southeastern Alaska. Pat Roppel, longtime Southeast resident and expert on the region's history, examines in detail the past and present of Sitka, Baranof Island, and neighboring Chichagof Island. Illustrated with contemporary color and historical black-and-white photographs. 128 pages, $9.95.

Wrangell-Saint Elias, Vol. 8, No. 1. Mountains, including the continent's second- and fourth-highest peaks, dominate this international wilderness that sweeps from the Wrangell Mountains in Alaska to the southern Saint Elias range in Canada. Illustrated with contemporary color and historical black-and-white photographs. Includes a large fold-out map. 144 pages, $9.95.

Alaska National Interest Lands, Vol. 8, No. 4. Following passage of the bill formalizing Alaska's national interest land selections (d-2 lands), longtime Alaskans Celia Hunter and Ginny Wood review each selection, outlining location, size, access, and briefly describing the region's special attractions. Illustrated with contemporary color photographs. 242 pages, $14.95.

Islands of the Seals: The Pribilofs, Vol. 9, No. 3.
Great herds of northern fur seals drew Russians and
Aleuts to these remote Bering Sea islands where they
founded permanent communities and established a
unique international commerce. Illustrated with
contemporary color and historical black-and-white
photographs. 128 pages, $9.95.

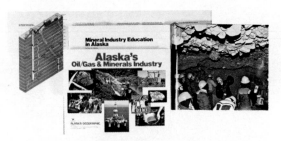

**Alaska's Oil/Gas & Minerals Industry, Vol. 9,
No. 4.** Experts detail the geological processes and
resulting mineral and fossil fuel resources that are
now in the forefront of Alaska's economy.
Illustrated with historical black-and-white and
contemporary color photographs. 216 pages,
$12.95.

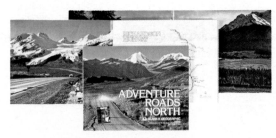

**Adventure Roads North: The Story of the
Alaska Highway and Other Roads in** *The
MILEPOST* ®, **Vol. 10, No. 1.** From Alaska's first
highway — the Richardson — to the famous
Alaska Highway, first overland route to the
49th state, text and photos provide a history of
Alaska's roads and take a mile-by-mile look at the
country they cross. 224 pages, $14.95.

**ANCHORAGE and the Cook Inlet Basin . . .
Alaska's Commercial Heartland, Vol. 10, No. 2.**
An update of what's going on in "Anchorage
country" . . . the Kenai, the Susitna Valley, and
Matanuska. Heavily illustrated in color and
including three illustrated maps . . . one an
uproarious artist's forecast of "Anchorage 2035."
168 pages, $14.95.

Alaska's Salmon Fisheries, Vol. 10, No. 3.
The work of *ALASKA* ® magazine Outdoors Editor
Jim Rearden, this issue takes a comprehensive
look at Alaska's most valuable commercial fishery.
Through text and photos, readers will learn about
the five species of salmon caught in Alaska,
different types of fishing gear and how each works,
and will take a district-by-district tour of salmon
fisheries throughout the state. 128 pages, $12.95.

NEXT ISSUE.
   **Nome: City of the Golden Beaches, Vol. 11,
No. 1.** The colorful history of Alaska's most
famous gold rush town has never been told like
this before. With a text written by Terrence Cole,
and illustrated with hundreds of rare black and
white photos, the book traces the story of Nome
from the crazy days of the 1900 gold rush. To
members in February 1984. Price to be
announced.

The Alaska Geographic Society

Box 4-EEE, Anchorage, AK 99509

   Membership in The Alaska Geographic Society
is $30, which includes the following year's four
quarterlies which explore a wide variety of
subjects in the Northland, each issue an adventure
in great photos, maps, and excellent research.
Members receive their quarterlies as part of the
membership fee at considerable savings over the
prices which nonmembers must pay for individual
book editions.